HISTORY & GEOGRAPHY 400
Teacher's Guide

Author:

Theresa K. Buskey, B.A., J.D.

Editor:

Alan Christopherson, M.S.

804 N. 2nd Ave. E.,
Rock Rapids, IA 51246-1759

HISTORY & GEOGRAPHY 400

LIFEPAC® Overview

HISTORY & GEOGRAPHY SCOPE & SEQUENCE

	Grade 1	Grade 2	Grade 3
UNIT 1	I AM A SPECIAL PERSON • God made me • All about you • Using proper manners	LOOKING BACK • Remembering last year • Learning about early times • The trail of the Native Americans • Symbols and historic places	U.S. GEOGRAPHY AND HISTORY STUDY SKILLS • Map skills • Resources • Community
UNIT 2	COMMUNICATING WITH SOUND • Sounds people make • Sounds that communicate • Communicating without sound • Communicating with God	SETTLING THE NEW WORLD • The first settlers • Colonies of the new world • War for Independence • Symbols and historical places	NEW ENGLAND STATES • ME, NH, VT, MA, RI, AND CT • New England geography • New England resources • New England community
UNIT 3	I HAVE FEELINGS • I feel sad • I feel afraid • I feel happy • I have other feelings	A NEW GOVERNMENT FOR A NEW COUNTRY • A study of government • Creating a government • Our government • Symbols and historical places	MID-ATLANTIC STATES • NY, PA, NJ, DE, MD, and DC • Mid-Atlantic geography • Mid-Atlantic resources • Mid-Atlantic community
UNIT 4	I LIVE IN A FAMILY • My mother and father • My brothers and sisters • My grandparents • What my family does	GOVERNMENT UNDER THE CONSTITUTION • Article One–The Legislative Branch • Article Two–The Executive Branch • Article Three–The Judicial Branch • The Bill of Rights • Symbols and historical places	SOUTHERN ATLANTIC STATES • WV, VA, NC, SC, GA, AND FL • Southern Atlantic geography • Southern Atlantic resources • Southern Atlantic community
UNIT 5	YOU AND GOD'S FAMILY • Getting ready in the morning • Walking to school • The school family • The church family	OUR GOVERNMENT CLOSE TO HOME • Our state governments • Our local governments • Citizens of the United States • Symbols and historical places	SOUTHERN STATES • KY, TN, MS, LA, AL, OK, TX, AND AR • Southern geography • Southern resources • Southern community
UNIT 6	PLACES PEOPLE LIVE • Life on the farm • Life in the city • Life by the sea	WESTWARD–FROM THE ORIGINAL COLONIES • The United States grows • The Lewis and Clark expedition • The Old Southwest • Symbols and historical places	GREAT LAKES STATES • OH, IN, IL, MI, WI, and MN • Great Lakes geography • Great Lakes resources • Great Lakes community
UNIT 7	COMMUNITY HELPERS • Firefighters and police officers • Doctors • City workers • Teachers and ministers	SETTLING THE FRONTIER • The Texas frontier • Westward expansion • Meet America's pioneers • Symbols and historical places	MIDWESTERN STATES • ND, SD, NE, KS, MO, and IA • Midwestern geography • Midwestern resources • Midwestern community
UNIT 8	I LOVE MY COUNTRY • America discovered • The Pilgrims • The United States begin • Respect for your country	EXPLORING AMERICA WITH MAPS • Directions on a map • Reading roads and symbols • Natural features • Symbols and historical places	MOUNTAIN STATES • MT, ID, WY, NV, UT, CO, AZ, and NM • Mountain geography • Mountain resources • Mountain community
UNIT 9	I LIVE IN THE WORLD • The globe • Countries • Friends in Mexico • Friends in Japan	PAST, PRESENT, AND FUTURE MAPS • City maps • Building maps • History of maps • Symbols and historical places	PACIFIC STATES • WA, OR, CA, AK, and HI • Pacific geography • Pacific resources • Pacific community
UNIT 10	THE WORLD AND YOU • You are special • Your family • Your school and church • Your world	REVIEW UNITED STATES HISTORY • The United States begins • Creating a government • Mapping the United States	U.S. GEOGRAPHY AND HISTORY REVIEW • U.S. geographical features • Eastern U.S. review • Western U.S. review

HISTORY & GEOGRAPHY SCOPE & SEQUENCE

Grade 4	Grade 5	Grade 6	
OUR EARTH • The surface of the earth • Early explorations of the earth • Exploring from space • Exploring the oceans	**A NEW WORLD** • Exploration of America • The first colonies • Conflict with Britain • Birth of the United States	**WORLD GEOGRAPHY** • Latitude and longitude • Western and eastern hemispheres • The southern hemisphere • Political and cultural regions	UNIT 1
SEAPORT CITIES • Sydney • Hong Kong • Istanbul • London	**A NEW NATION** • War for Independence • Life in America • A new form of government • The Nation's early years	**THE CRADLE OF CIVILIZATION** • Mesopotamia • The land of Israel • The Nation of Israel • Egypt	UNIT 2
DESERT LANDS • What is a desert? • Where are the deserts? • How do people live in the desert?	**A TIME OF TESTING** • Louisiana Purchase • War of 1812 • Sectionalism • Improvements in trade & travel	**GREECE AND ROME** • Geography of the region • Beginning civilizations • Contributions to other civilizations • The influence of Christianity	UNIT 3
GRASSLANDS • Grasslands of the world • Ukraine • Kenya • Argentina	**A GROWING NATION** • Andrew Jackson's influence • Texas & Oregon • Mexican War • The Nation divides	**THE MIDDLE AGES** • The feudal system • Books and schools • The Crusades • Trade and architecture	UNIT 4
TROPICAL RAIN FORESTS • Facts about rain forests • Rain forests of the world • The Amazon rain forest • The Congo rain forest	**A DIVIDED NATION** • Civil War • Reconstruction • Gilded Age • The need for reform	**SIX SOUTH AMERICAN COUNTRIES** • Brazil • Colombia • Venezuela • Three Guianas	UNIT 5
THE POLAR REGIONS • The polar regions: coldest places in the world • The Arctic polar region • The Antarctic polar region	**A CHANGING NATION** • Progressive reforms • Spanish-American War • World War I • Roaring Twenties	**OTHER AMERICAN COUNTRIES** • Ecuador and Peru • Bolivia and Uruguay • Paraguay and Argentina • Chile	UNIT 6
MOUNTAIN COUNTRIES • Peru – the Andes • The Incas and modern Peru • Nepal – the Himalayas • Switzerland – the Alps	**DEPRESSION AND WAR** • The Great Depression • War begins in Europe • War in Europe • War in the Pacific	**AFRICA** • Geography and cultures • Countries of northern Africa • Countries of central Africa • Countries of southern Africa	UNIT 7
ISLAND COUNTRIES • Islands of the earth • Cuba • Iceland • Japan	**COLD WAR** • Korean War & other crises • Vietnam War • Civil Rights movement • Upheaval in America	**MODERN WESTERN EUROPE** • The Renaissance • The Industrial Revolution • World War I • World War II	UNIT 8
NORTH AMERICA • Geography • Lands, lakes, and rivers • Northern countries • Southern countries	**INTO THE NEW MILLENNIUM** • Watergate and détente • The fall of communism • The Persian Gulf • Issues of the new millennium	**MODERN EASTERN EUROPE** • Early government • Early churches • Early countries • Modern countries	UNIT 9
OUR WORLD IN REVIEW • Europe and the explorers • Asia and Africa • Southern continents • North America, North Pole	**THE UNITED STATES OF AMERICA** • Beginning America until 1830 • Stronger America 1830-1930 • 1930 to the end of the millennium • The new millennium	**THE DEVELOPMENT OF OUR WORLD** • Cradle of civilization • The Middle Ages • Modern Europe • South America and Africa	UNIT 10

HISTORY & GEOGRAPHY SCOPE & SEQUENCE

	Grade 7	Grade 8	Grade 9
UNIT 1	WHAT IS HISTORY • Definition and significance of history • Historians and the historical method • Views of history	EUROPE COMES TO AMERICA • Voyages of Columbus • Spanish exploration • Other exploration • The first colonies	UNITED STATES HERITAGE • American colonies • Acquisitions and annexations • Backgrounds to freedom • Backgrounds to society
UNIT 2	WHAT IS GEOGRAPHY • Classes of geography • Geography and relief of the earth • Maps and the study of our world • Time zones	BRITISH AMERICA • English colonies • Government • Lifestyle • Wars with France	OUR NATIONAL GOVERNMENT • Ideals of national government • National government developed • Legislative and Executive branches • Judicial branch
UNIT 3	U.S. HISTORY AND GEOGRAPHY • Geography of the U.S. • Early history of the U.S. • Physical regions of the U.S. • Cultural regions of the U.S.	THE AMERICAN REVOLUTION • British control • Rebellion of the Colonies • War for Independence • Constitution	STATE AND LOCAL GOVERNMENT • Powers of state government • County government • Township government • City government
UNIT 4	ANTHROPOLOGY • Understanding anthropology • The unity of man • The diversity of man • The culture of man	A FIRM FOUNDATION • Washington's presidency • Adams administration • Jeffersonian Democracy • War of 1812	PLANNING A CAREER • Definition of a career • God's will concerning a career • Selecting a career • Preparation for a career
UNIT 5	SOCIOLOGY • Sociology defined • Historical development • Importance to Christians • Method of sociology	A GROWING NATION • Jacksonian Era • Northern border • Southern border • Industrial Revolution	CITIZENSHIP • Citizenship defined • Gaining citizenship • Rights of citizenship • Responsibilities of citizenship
UNIT 6	U.S. ANTHROPOLOGY • Cultural background of the U.S. • Native American cultures • Cultures from distant lands • Cultural and social interaction	THE CIVIL WAR • Division & Secession • Civil War • Death of Lincoln • Reconstruction	THE EARTH AND MAN • Man inhabits the earth • Man's home on the earth • Man develops the earth • The future of the earth
UNIT 7	ECONOMICS • Economics defined • Methods of the economist • Tools of the economist • An experiment in economy	GILDED AGE TO PROGRESSIVE ERA • Rise of industry • Wild West • America as a world power • Progressive era	REGIONS OF THE WORLD • A region defined • Geographic and climate regions • Cultural and political regions • Economic regions of Europe
UNIT 8	POLITICAL SCIENCE • Definition of political science • Roots of Western thought • Modern political thinkers • Political theory	A WORLD IN CONFLICT • World War I • Great Depression • New Deal • World War II	MAN AND HIS ENVIRONMENT • The physical environment • Drug abuse • The social environment • Man's responsibilities
UNIT 9	STATE ECONOMICS AND POLITICS • Background of state government • State government • State finance • State politics	COLD WAR AMERICA • Origins of the Cold War • Vietnam • Truman to Nixon • Ending of the Cold War	TOOLS OF THE GEOGRAPHER • The globe • Types of maps • Reading maps • The earth in symbol form
UNIT 10	SOCIAL SCIENCES REVIEW • History and geography • Anthropology • Sociology • Economics and politics	RECENT AMERICA & REVIEW • Europe to Independence • Colonies to the Civil War • Civil War to World War II • World War II through Cold War	MAN IN A CHANGING WORLD • Development of the nation • Development of government • Development of the earth • Solving problems

HISTORY & GEOGRAPHY SCOPE & SEQUENCE

Grade 10	Grade 11	Grade 12	
ANCIENT CIVILIZATION • Origin of civilization • Early Egypt • Assyria and Babylonia • Persian civilization	FOUNDATIONS OF DEMOCRACY • Democracy develops • Virginia • New England colonies • Middle and southern colonies	INTERNATIONAL GOVERNMENTS • Why have governments • Types of governments • Governments in our world • Political thinkers	UNIT 1
ANCIENT CIVILIZATIONS • India • China • Greek civilization • Roman Empire	CONSTITUTIONAL GOVERNMENT • Relations with England • The Revolutionary War • Articles of Confederation • Constitution of the U.S.	UNITED STATES GOVERNMENT • U.S. Constitution • Bill of Rights • Three branches of government • Legislative process	UNIT 2
THE MEDIEVAL WORLD • Early Middle Ages • Middle Ages in transition • High Middle Ages	NATIONAL EXPANSION • A strong federal government • Revolution of 1800 • War of 1812 • Nationalism and sectionalism	AMERICAN PARTY SYSTEM • American party system • Development of political parties • Functions of political parties • Voting	UNIT 3
RENAISSANCE AND REFORMATION • Changes in government and art • Changes in literature and thought • Advances in science • Reform within the Church	A NATION DIVIDED • Issues of division • Division of land and people • Economics of slavery • Politics of slavery	HISTORY OF GOVERNMENTS • Primitive governments • Beginnings of Democracy • Feudalism, Theocracy & Democracy • Fascism & Nazism	UNIT 4
GROWTH OF WORLD EMPIRES • England and France • Portugal and Spain • Austria and Germany • Italy and the Ottoman Empire	A NATION UNITED AGAIN • Regionalism • The Division • The Civil War • Reconstruction	THE CHRISTIAN & GOVERNMENT • Discrimination & the Christian • Christian attitudes • "Opinion & Truth" in politics • Politics & Propaganda	UNIT 5
THE AGE OF REVOLUTION • Factors leading to revolution • The English Revolution • The American Revolution • The French Revolution	INVOLVEMENT AT HOME & ABROAD • Surge of industry • The industrial lifestyle • Isolationism • Involvement in conflict	FREE ENTERPRISE • Economics • Competition • Money through history • International finance & currency	UNIT 6
THE INDUSTRIAL REVOLUTION • Sparks of preparation • Industrial revolution in England • Industrial revolution in America • Social changes of the revolution	THE SEARCH FOR PEACE • The War and its aftermath • The Golden Twenties • The Great Depression • The New Deal	BUSINESS AND YOU • Running a business • Government & Business • Banks & Mergers • Deregulation & Bankruptcy	UNIT 7
TWO WORLD WARS • Mounting tension • World War I • Peace and power quests • World War II	A NATION AT WAR • Causes of the war • World War II • Korean Conflict • Vietnam Conflict	THE STOCK MARKET • How it started and works • Selecting stocks • Types of stocks • Tracking stocks	UNIT 8
THE CONTEMPORARY WORLD • The Cold War • Korean War and Vietnam War • Collapse of the Soviet Union • Today's world	CONTEMPORARY AMERICA • America in the 1960s • America in the 1970s • America in the 80s & 90s • International scene 1980-present	BUDGET AND FINANCE • Cash, Credit & Checking • Buying a car • Grants, Loans & IRAs • Savings & E-cash	UNIT 9
ANCIENT TIMES TO THE PRESENT • Ancient civilizations • Medieval times • The Renaissance • The modern world	UNITED STATES HISTORY • Basis of democracy • The 1800s • Industrialization • Current history	GEOGRAPHY AND REVIEW • Euro & International finance • U.S. Geography • The global traveler • Neighbors, Heroes & The Holy Land	UNIT 10

STRUCTURE OF THE LIFEPAC CURRICULUM

The LIFEPAC curriculum is conveniently structured to provide one teacher's guide containing teacher support material with answer keys and ten student worktexts for each subject at grade levels two through twelve. The worktext format of the LIFEPACs allows the student to read the textual information and complete workbook activities all in the same booklet. The easy to follow LIFEPAC numbering system lists the grade as the first number(s) and the last two digits as the number of the series. For example, the Language Arts LIFEPAC at the 6th grade level, 5th book in the series would be LAN0605.

Each LIFEPAC is divided into 3 to 5 sections and begins with an introduction or overview of the booklet as well as a series of specific learning objectives to give a purpose to the study of the LIFEPAC. The introduction and objectives are followed by a vocabulary section which may be found at the beginning of each section at the lower levels or in the glossary at the high school level. Vocabulary words are used to develop word recognition and should not be confused with the spelling words introduced later in the LIFEPAC. The student should learn all vocabulary words before working the LIFEPAC sections to improve comprehension, retention, and reading skills.

Each activity or written assignment has a number for easy identification, such as 1.1. The first number corresponds to the LIFEPAC section and the number to the right of the decimal is the number of the activity.

Teacher checkpoints, which are essential to maintain quality learning, are found at various locations throughout the LIFEPAC. The teacher should check 1) neatness of work and penmanship, 2) quality of understanding (tested with a short oral quiz), 3) thoroughness of answers (complete sentences and paragraphs, correct spelling, etc.), 4) completion of activities (no blank spaces), and 5) accuracy of answers as compared to the answer key (all answers correct).

The self test questions are also number coded for easy reference. For example, 2.015 means that this is the 15th question in the self test of Section 2. The first number corresponds to the LIFEPAC section, the zero indicates that it is a self test question, and the number to the right of the zero the question number.

The LIFEPAC test is packaged at the centerfold of each LIFEPAC. It should be removed and put aside before giving the booklet to the student for study.

Answer and test keys have the same numbering system as the LIFEPACs. The student may be given access to the answer keys (not the test keys) under teacher supervision so that he can score his own work.

A thorough study of the LIFEPAC Overview by the teacher before instruction begins is essential to the success of the student. The teacher should become familiar with expected skill mastery and understand how these grade-level skills fit into the overall skill development of the curriculum. The teacher should also preview the objectives that appear at the beginning of each LIFEPAC for additional preparation and planning.

TEST SCORING AND GRADING

Answer keys and test keys give examples of correct answers. They convey the idea, but the student may use many ways to express a correct answer. The teacher should check for the essence of the answer, not for the exact wording. Many questions are high level and require thinking and creativity on the part of the student. Each answer should be scored based on whether or not the main idea written by the student matches the model example. "Any Order" or "Either Order" in a key indicates that no particular order is necessary to be correct.

Most self tests and LIFEPAC tests at the lower elementary levels are scored at 1 point per answer; however, the upper levels may have a point system awarding 2 to 5 points for various answers or questions. Further, the total test points will vary; they may not always equal 100 points. They may be 78, 85, 100, 105, etc.

Example 1

Example 2

A score box similar to ex. 1 above is located at the end of each self test and on the front of the LIFEPAC test. The bottom score, 72, represents the total number of points possible on the test. The upper score, 58, represents the number of points your student will need to receive an 80% or passing grade. If you wish to establish the exact percentage that your student has achieved, find the total points of his correct answers and divide it by the bottom number (in this case 72). For example, if your student has a point total of 65, divide 65 by 72 for a grade of 90%. Referring to ex. 2, on a test with a total of 105 possible points, the student would have to receive a minimum of 84 correct points for an 80% or passing grade. If your student has received 93 points, simply divide the 93 by 105 for a percentage grade of 89%. Students who receive a score below 80% should review the LIFEPAC and retest using the appropriate Alternate Test found in the Teacher's Guide.

The following is a guideline to assign letter grades for completed LIFEPACs based on a maximum total score of 100 points.

Example:

LIFEPAC Test	=	60% of the Total Score (or percent grade)
Self Test	=	25% of the Total Score (average percent of self tests)
Reports	=	10% or 10* points per LIFEPAC
Oral Work	=	5% or 5* points per LIFEPAC

*Determined by the teacher's subjective evaluation of the student's daily work.

Example:

LIFEPAC Test Score	=	92%	92 x .60	=	55 points
Self Test Average	=	90%	90 x .25	=	23 points
Reports				=	8 points
Oral Work				=	4 points

TOTAL POINTS	=	90 points

Grade Scale based on point system:

100 – 94	=	A
93 – 86	=	B
85 – 77	=	C
76 – 70	=	D
Below 70	=	F

TEACHER HINTS AND STUDYING TECHNIQUES

LIFEPAC activities are written to check the level of understanding of the preceding text. The student may look back to the text as necessary to complete these activities; however, a student should never attempt to do the activities without reading (studying) the text first. Self tests and LIFEPAC tests are never open book tests.

Language arts activities (skill integration) often appear within other subject curriculum. The purpose is to give the student an opportunity to test his skill mastery outside of the context in which it was presented.

Writing complete answers (paragraphs) to some questions is an integral part of the LIFEPAC curriculum in all subjects. This builds communication and organization skills, increases understanding and retention of ideas, and helps enforce good penmanship. Complete sentences should be encouraged for this type of activity. Obviously, single words or phrases do not meet the intent of the activity, since multiple lines are given for the response.

Review is essential to student success. Time invested in review where review is suggested will be time saved in correcting errors later. Self tests, unlike the section activities, are closed book. This procedure helps to identify weaknesses before they become too great to overcome. Certain objectives from self tests are cumulative and test previous sections; therefore, good preparation for a self test must include all material studied up to that testing point.

The following procedure checklist has been found to be successful in developing good study habits in the LIFEPAC curriculum.

1. Read the introduction and Table of Contents.
2. Read the objectives.
3. Recite and study the entire vocabulary (glossary) list.
4. Study each section as follows:
   a. Read the introduction and study the section objectives.
   b. Read all the text for the entire section, but answer none of the activities.
   c. Return to the beginning of the section and memorize each vocabulary word and definition.
   d. Reread the section, complete the activities, check the answers with the answer key, correct all errors, and have the teacher check.
   e. Read the self test but do not answer the questions.
   f. Go to the beginning of the first section and reread the text and answers to the activities up to the self test you have not yet done.
   g. Answer the questions to the self test without looking back.
   h. Have the self test checked by the teacher.
   i. Correct the self test and have the teacher check the corrections.
   j. Repeat steps a–i for each section.
5. Use the SQ3R method to prepare for the LIFEPAC test.
   Scan the whole LIFEPAC.
   Question yourself on the objectives.
   Read the whole LIFEPAC again.
   Recite through an oral examination.
   Review weak areas.
6. Take the LIFEPAC test as a closed book test.
7. LIFEPAC tests are administered and scored under direct teacher supervision. Students who receive scores below 80% should review the LIFEPAC using the SQ3R study method and take the Alternate Test located in the Teacher's Guide. The final test grade may be the grade on the Alternate Test or an average of the grades from the original LIFEPAC test and the Alternate Test.

GOAL SETTING AND SCHEDULES

Each school must develop its own schedule, because no single set of procedures will fit every situation. The following is an example of a daily schedule that includes the five LIFEPAC subjects as well as time slotted for special activities.

Possible Daily Schedule

8:15 – 8:25	Pledges, prayer, songs, devotions, etc.
8:25 – 9:10	Bible
9:10 – 9:55	Language Arts
9:55 – 10:15	Recess (juice break)
10:15 – 11:00	Math
11:00 – 11:45	History & Geography
11:45 – 12:30	Lunch, recess, quiet time
12:30 – 1:15	Science
1:15 –	Drill, remedial work, enrichment*

Enrichment: *Computer time, physical education, field trips, fun reading, games and puzzles, family business, hobbies, resource persons, guests, crafts, creative work, electives, music appreciation, projects.*

Basically, two factors need to be considered when assigning work to a student in the LIFEPAC curriculum.

The first is time. An average of 45 minutes should be devoted to each subject, each day. Remember, this is only an average. Because of extenuating circumstances a student may spend only 15 minutes on a subject one day and the next day spend 90 minutes on the same subject.

The second factor is the number of pages to be worked in each subject. A single LIFEPAC is designed to take 3 to 4 weeks to complete. Allowing about 3 to 4 days for LIFEPAC introduction, review, and tests, the student has approximately 15 days to complete the LIFEPAC pages. Simply take the number of pages in the LIFEPAC, divide it by 15 and you will have the number of pages that must be completed on a daily basis to keep the student on schedule. For example, a LIFEPAC containing 45 pages will require 3 completed pages per day. Again, this is only an average. While working a 45 page LIFEPAC, the student may complete only 1 page the first day if the text has a lot of activities or reports, but go on to complete 5 pages the next day.

Long-range planning requires some organization. Because the traditional school year originates in the early fall of one year and continues to late spring of the following year, a calendar should be devised that covers this period of time. Approximate beginning and completion dates can be noted on the calendar as well as special occasions such as holidays, vacations and birthdays. Since each LIFEPAC takes 3 to 4 weeks or eighteen days to complete, it should take about 180 school days to finish a set of ten LIFEPACs. Starting at the beginning school date, mark off eighteen school days on the calendar and that will become the targeted completion date for the first LIFEPAC. Continue marking the calendar until you have established dates for the remaining nine LIFEPACs making adjustments for previously noted holidays and vacations. If all five subjects are being used, the ten established target dates should be the same for the LIFEPACs in each subject.

TEACHING SUPPLEMENTS

The sample weekly lesson plan and student grading sheet forms are included in this section as teacher support materials and may be duplicated at the convenience of the teacher.

The student grading sheet is provided for those who desire to follow the suggested guidelines for assignment of letter grades as previously discussed. The student's self test scores should be posted as percentage grades. When the LIFEPAC is completed the teacher should average the self test grades, multiply the average by .25 and post the points in the box marked self test points. The LIFEPAC percentage grade should be multiplied by .60 and posted. Next, the teacher should award and post points for written reports and oral work. A report may be any type of written work assigned to the student whether it is a LIFEPAC or additional learning activity. Oral work includes the student's ability to respond orally to questions which may or may not be related to LIFEPAC activities or any type of oral report assigned by the teacher. The points may then be totaled and a final grade entered along with the date that the LIFEPAC was completed.

The Student Record Book, which was specifically designed for use with the Alpha Omega curriculum, provides space to record weekly progress for one student over a nine-week period as well as a place to post self test and LIFEPAC scores. The Student Record Books are available through the current Alpha Omega catalog; however, unlike the enclosed forms these books are not for duplication and should be purchased in sets of four to cover a full academic year.

WEEKLY LESSON PLANNER

Week of:

	Subject	Subject	Subject	Subject
Monday				
Tuesday	Subject	Subject	Subject	Subject
Wednesday	Subject	Subject	Subject	Subject
Thursday	Subject	Subject	Subject	Subject
Friday	Subject	Subject	Subject	Subject

WEEKLY LESSON PLANNER

Week of:

	Subject	Subject	Subject	Subject
Monday				
Tuesday				
Wednesday				
Thursday				
Friday				

Student Name _____   Year _____

Bible

LP #	Self Test Scores by Sections					Self Test Points	LIFEPAC Test	Oral Points	Report Points	Final Grade	Date
	1	2	3	4	5						
01											
02											
03											
04											
05											
06											
07											
08											
09											
10											

History & Geography

LP #	Self Test Scores by Sections					Self Test Points	LIFEPAC Test	Oral Points	Report Points	Final Grade	Date
	1	2	3	4	5						
01											
02											
03											
04											
05											
06											
07											
08											
09											
10											

Language Arts

LP #	Self Test Scores by Sections					Self Test Points	LIFEPAC Test	Oral Points	Report Points	Final Grade	Date
	1	2	3	4	5						
01											
02											
03											
04											
05											
06											
07											
08											
09											
10											

Student Name _____   Year _____

Math

LP #	Self Test Scores by Sections					Self Test Points	LIFEPAC Test	Oral Points	Report Points	Final Grade	Date
	1	2	3	4	5						
01											
02											
03											
04											
05											
06											
07											
08											
09											
10											

Science

LP #	Self Test Scores by Sections					Self Test Points	LIFEPAC Test	Oral Points	Report Points	Final Grade	Date
	1	2	3	4	5						
01											
02											
03											
04											
05											
06											
07											
08											
09											
10											

Spelling/Electives

LP #	Self Test Scores by Sections					Self Test Points	LIFEPAC Test	Oral Points	Report Points	Final Grade	Date
	1	2	3	4	5						
01											
02											
03											
04											
05											
06											
07											
08											
09											
10											

INSTRUCTIONS FOR HISTORY & GEOGRAPHY

The LIFEPAC curriculum from grades two through twelve is structured so that the daily instructional material is written directly into the LIFEPACs. The student is encouraged to read and follow this instructional material in order to develop independent study habits. The teacher should introduce the LIFEPAC to the student, set a required completion schedule, complete teacher checks, be available for questions regarding both content and procedures, administer and grade tests, and develop additional learning activities as desired. Teachers working with several students may schedule their time so that students are assigned to a quiet work activity when it is necessary to spend instructional time with one particular student.

This fourth grade curriculum is an adventure in geography. The intent of the course is to introduce the student to the geography of the world. The student will be exposed to geography terms like peninsula, archipelago, hemisphere and isthmus. The use of this terminology will give the student the vocabulary they need to discuss and understand geography. These terms will be introduced in the first LIFEPAC along with a quick history of the exploration of our earth. Later LIFEPACs will build on this foundation, continuing to use the new terms and introducing others.

Each LIFEPAC in 402–408 will take the student on a trip to different parts of the world exploring a specific type of climate or land form, such as deserts, mountains or islands. The student will learn about nations or areas in different parts of the world that share those specific characteristics. The theme of the LIFEPAC (islands, seaports, rain forests, etc.) will be used as a medium to introduce the student to life in several different places or nations, in different parts of our world, that share that fall under that theme. Culture, people, crops, animals, transportation, traditional life, religion and products will be among the topics discussed for each nation or region. This will introduce the students to the wide expanse of world geography.

LIFEPAC 409 will focus on the continent of North America. It will use the student's new knowledge of different climates and land forms to show how God put them together on one particular continent, our own. This LIFEPAC will also discuss nations, history, people and culture in a more limited fashion. The last LIFEPAC will continue this trend by reviewing for the entire year, not by topic again, but by continent. Instead of all the deserts of the world, the review will present one continent, such as Africa, and review the deserts, islands, seaports, etc. that are on that continent.

Thus, by the end of the year the student should have a "bare bones" introduction to the climates, land forms and continents of the world. It is beyond the scope of this year's curriculum to learn the all nations of the world. There are just too many. This curriculum concentrates on a few representative nations and thereby introduces the student to such varied topics as trade, Hinduism, forest conservation, communism, drought, famine, ancient civilizations and colonialism. This is an introductory course that will hopefully lead the student into a life-long curiosity about the varied peoples and lands of our earth. For this purpose a general state history activity is located on the following pages.

This course is intended to be challenging for a fourth grader. The teacher should feel free to eliminate some of the outside activities to fit with the needs of the students or the goals of the instructor. Equally, activities can be added that are of particular interest to the instructor/student. This year is meant to be a geographic adventure that will supply the student with a basis for expanding his or her knowledge of geography as they grow.

HISTORY & GEOGRAPHY 401

Unit 1: Our Earth

TEACHER NOTES

MATERIALS NEEDED FOR LIFEPAC	
Required	Suggested
• dictionary • encyclopedia • atlas, maps, globe • pictures or videos of space travel or exploration • crayons, colored pencils or markers (the reference materials can be either in book or online formats)	• any books and magazines about space travel, exploration, and underwater discoveries • spices: peppercorns and pepper mill • pictures of fifteenth- and sixteenth-century sailing ships • paste and scissors • pictures (if available) of spaceships, astronauts, earth as seen from outer space, scuba divers, underwater explorations, and so forth

ADDITIONAL LEARNING ACTIVITIES

Section 1: The Surface of the Earth

1. Map drills. Introduce the geographical FISH POND. Get a plastic dishpan for the pond. Cut strips of tag board about 2" x 10" and print names on them of important places in the world. (Use the places mentioned in the LIFEPAC and others the children suggest.) Put a paper clip on each tag strip for the "mouth of the fish." Get two or three tree branches or sticks about a yard long and tie a string to each. Fasten a magnetized hook or bar magnet to each fish line. The pond is ready for fishermen. Let the children fish. If they catch a tag they must locate the place on the world map or globe within a minute, or so, otherwise a new fisherman is chosen. Later the children can fish on their own in small groups when they have "free" time.

2. Make a world map showing the seven continents and four large oceans. Color and label.

3. Some students could make a globe of paper mache and paint on it the continents and oceans and label them. Paper mache can be made by mixing paste (wallpaper or library paste or liquid starch), dipping strips of newspaper through it, and wrapping the strips around a frame. The frame for a globe could be a blown up balloon or a paper bag stuffed with crumpled paper.

Section 2: Early Explorations of Our Earth

1. Show the class a peppercorn and peel off some of the black skin. Let them try making white pepper out of the black berries. Let them grind some in a pepper mill.

2. Two or more students could prepare a report on several spices. The report could include where the spice comes from, what it is used for, what taste it has, and a sample put on a chart. The chart of samples could also include a drawing of the spice as a growing plant and also as it looks in the can purchased from the grocery store.

3. Make a model of the Santa Maria or another explorer's ship.

4. Have a student plan a chart on spice samples, where the spice came from, and how it is used.

5. Have a student write down the qualities that helped make one of the explorers successful.

6. A student could make a map showing journeys of Columbus, Marco Polo, or Magellan.

Section 3: Recent Explorations of Our Earth

1. Have the students bring in news items on space shuttles, weather satellites, and so forth.

2. If some students are especially interested in oceanography, they might draw and label an underwater scene complete with divers, *Trieste*, plants, fish, and treasures. This idea could be expanded into a diorama with an accompanying report.

3. Students could prepare a bulletin board display of pictures and news stories about space and ocean exploration.

Have a student report on the current news or programs about undersea explorations. Discussion of these programs would increase interest as well as knowledge.

4. Some students may enjoy constructing a model of one of the many exploratory space vehicles. A short report explaining a little about the mission and crew of the space shuttle could be written also.

5. Draw and color a picture of the earth as seen from the moon.

Administer the LIFEPAC Test.

The test is to be administered in one session. Give no help except with directions.
Evaluate the tests and review areas where the students have done poorly.
Review the pages and activities that stress the concepts tested.
If necessary, administer the Alternate LIFEPAC Test.

ANSWER KEYS

SECTION 1

1.1 Any order: Africa, Asia, Europe, North America, South America, Australia, Antarctica

1.2 Pacific, Atlantic, Indian, Arctic

1.3-1.7 Teacher check

1.8 globe

1.9 sphere

1.10 equator

1.11 Any order: Cancer, Capricorn

1.12 Southern

1.13 Northern

1.14 north

1.15 south

1.16 east

1.17 north

1.18 west

1.19 1. Pacific
2. Atlantic
3. Indian
4. Arctic

1.20 day

1.21 South Pole

1.22 Atlantic Ocean; Mediterranean Sea

1.23 harbors

1.24 Three-fourths

1.25 imaginary

1.26 Hudson Bay

1.27 Asia

1.28 seven

1.29 Antarctica

1.30 Europe

1.31 Isthmus of Panama

1.32 Africa

1.33 Any order: North America, South America

1.34 Eurasia

1.35-1.38 Teacher check

1.39 a

1.40 e

1.41 f

1.42 b

1.43 c

1.44 d

1.45 Baykal

1.46 Mississippi

1.47 Nile; Africa

1.48 Superior; North America

SELF TEST 1

1.01 1. h
2. a
3. k
4. j
5. d
6. b
7. e
8. i
9. g
10. c
11. f

1.02 g

1.03 a

1.04 j

1.05 i

1.06 f

1.07 h

1.08 b

1.09 c

1.010 e

1.011 d

1.012 a. north
b. west
c. south
d. east

1.013 hemisphere

1.014 globe

1.015 Nile

1.016 Cancer

1.017 Capricorn

1.018 fresh

1.019 Mississippi

1.020 axis

1.021 Superior

1.022 equator

1.023 true

1.024 false

1.025 true

1.026 false

1.027 false

1.028 false

1.029 true

1.030 true

SECTION 2

2.1	They were brought a very long way over a difficult route.
2.2	Spices grew in the warm islands and coasts of the Far East (India and the Spice Islands).
2.3	Pepper, cinnamon, nutmeg, and cloves were some of the valuable spices.
2.4	They could bring back large cargoes without having to pay to bring it across land.
2.5	No one knew a route to sail a ship to the Far East and people were afraid.
2.6	Teacher check
2.7	Navigator
2.8	Africa
2.9	Bartholomeu Dias
2.10	Vasco da Gama
2.11	build ships, sail, navigate, and make maps
2.12	further
2.13	false
2.14	false
2.15	true
2.16	false
2.17	true
2.18	false
2.19	true
2.20	Columbus' ships were named the *Niña*, the *Pinta*, and the *Santa Maria*.
2.21	The sailors were afraid they would not be able to get home against the wind.
2.22	Columbus thought he was near India and the West Indies were named for his mistake.
2.23	Columbus made four trips to the New World.
2.24	true
2.25	false
2.26	false
2.27	true
2.28	*Victoria*
2.29	Philippines; April 27, 1521
2.30	peaceful
2.31	King of Spain
2.32	very southern end of South America
2.33	Vasco de Balboa
2.34	a. sank near South America
	b. ran away back to Spain
	c. left behind in the Philippines
	d. had to return to the Spice Islands
2.35	eighteen
2.36	They learned the size, shape, and geography of the earth.

SELF TEST 2

2.01	B
2.02	J
2.03	A
2.04	G
2.05	C
2.06	D
2.07	F
2.08	H
2.09	I
2.010	E
2.011	C
2.012	H
2.013	M
2.014	C
2.015	C
2.016	M
2.017	C
2.018	H
2.019	M
2.020	H
2.021	d
2.022	c
2.023	e
2.024	h
2.025	f
2.026	a
2.027	i
2.028	g
2.029	b
2.030	j
2.031	They were brought a very long way over a difficult route.
2.032	They learned the size, shape, and geography of the earth.
2.033	smaller; the Americas
2.034	Spice Islands
2.035	Either order: Cancer, Capricorn

SECTION 3

3.1	Jacques Cousteau
3.2	continental shelf
3.3	Mariana Trench
3.4	bathysphere
3.5	mountain ridge
3.6	true
3.7	false
3.8	false
3.9	true
3.10	a. *Mercury*
	b. *Gemini*
	c. *Apollo*
3.11	astronauts; cosmonauts
3.12	Any order:
	Command Module, Lunar Module
3.13	*Apollo 11*
3.14	Any order:
	Neil Armstrong, Edwin Aldrin
3.15	Bible
3.16	Alan Shepard
3.17	John Glenn
3.18	World War II
3.19	a. 1
	b. 2
	c. 3
3.20	a. man-made object in space
	b. man in space
	c. woman in space
	d. space walk
3.21	the launch of *Sputnik*
3.22	a. *Mercury*
	b. *Gemini*
	c. *Apollo*
	d. Skylab
	e. Space Shuttle
3.23	fell from orbit
3.24	five to seven
3.25	Three
3.26	80
3.27	*Soyuz 19*
3.28	*Mir*
3.29	reused
3.30	Teacher check
3.31	hurricanes
3.32	Venus
3.33	phone
3.34	*Voyger*
3.35	lost
3.36	*Viking* I and II

SELF TEST 3

3.01	j
3.02	b
3.03	h
3.04	c
3.05	d
3.06	e
3.07	f
3.08	i
3.09	a
3.010	g
3.011	Mercury
3.012	Gemini
3.013	Apollo
3.014	Skylab
3.015	Space Shuttle
3.016	Apollo
3.017	Skylab
3.018	Mercury
3.019	Gemini
3.020	Space Shuttle
3.021	They have found what the ocean floor looks like, sunken ships, and sunken cities.
3.022	The Soviet Union and the United States raced to explore space.
3.023	A globe is the best map of the earth because it is the same shape as the real earth.
3.024	true
3.025	false
3.026	false
3.027	true
3.028	false
3.029	true
3.030	true
3.031	true
3.032	true
3.033	false
3.034	*Mir*
3.035	Pacific
3.036	Arctic
3.037	Vasco da Gama
3.038	equator
3.039	axis
3.040	hemisphere
3.041	peninsula
3.042	Spice Islands
3.043	Columbus

LIFEPAC TEST

1.	B	**24.-27.**	Any order:
2.	H	24.	Pacific
3.	G	25.	Atlantic
4.	J	26.	Indian
5.	C	27.	Arctic
6.	I	**28.-34.**	Any order:
7.	A	28.	Asia
8.	D	29.	Africa
9.	E	30.	Europe
10.	F	31.	Australia

(Give partial credit on 11-13)

11. They wanted to bring in spices without the problems of carrying them over land.
12. They learned the size, shape, and geography of the earth.
13. A globe is the best map of the earth because it is the same shape as the real earth.
14. North
15. East
16. equator
17. hemisphere
18. astronauts
19. b
20. d
21. c
22. e
23. a

32. North America
33. South America
34. Antarctica
35. Jacques Cousteau
36. Columbus
37. Voyager
38. Magellan
39. *Sputnik*
40. Vasco da Gama
41. Alan Shepard
42. Neil Armstrong
43. *Viking* I and II
44. Prince Henry
45. false
46. false
47. false
48. false
49. true
50. false

ALTERNATE LIFEPAC TEST

1.	C
2.	R
3.	C
4.	M
5.	O
6.	O
7.	O
8.	C
9.	C
10.	R
11.	M
12.	R
13.	R
14.	O
15.	C
16.	C
17.	R
18.	C
19.	M
20.	R
21.	g
22.	h
23.	a
24.	f
25.	d
26.	k
27.	n
28.	j

29. o
30. b
31. i
32. l
33. e
34. m
35. c

(Give partial credit on 36, 37, and 40)

36. Spices had to come a very long way over a difficult route.
37. It allows a diver to carry air on his back and move freely in the ocean.
38. a. north
    b. west
    c. south
    d. east
39. a. sea
    b. isthmus
    c. strait
    d. peninsula
40. They learned the size, shape, and geography of the earth.
41. false
42. true
43. false
44. false
45. true

HISTORY & GEOGRAPHY 401

ALTERNATE LIFEPAC TEST

NAME _____

DATE _____

SCORE _____

80

100

Put the correct letter next to each name (2 points each answer).

C - continent   O - ocean   R - name or part of a river   M - imaginary map line

1. _____ Asia

2. _____ Nile

3. _____ Australia

4. _____ axis

5. _____ Arctic

6. _____ Pacific

7. _____ Atlantic

8. _____ Africa

9. _____ South America

10. _____ delta

11. _____ equator

12. _____ Mississippi

13. _____ mouth

14. _____ Indian

15. _____ Antarctica

16. _____ Europe

17. _____ source

18. _____ North America

19. _____ Tropic of Cancer

20. _____ tributary

Choose the correct letter for the person or thing that matches each item listed below
(2 points each answer).

a. Prince Henry	b. Magellan	c. Columbus
d. Skylab	e. *Sputnik*	f. *Voyager*
g. Norsemen	h. Vasco da Gama	i. Viking I and II
j. *Mir*	k. Apollo	l. Mercury
m. Gemini	n. bathysphere	o. Space Shuttle

21. _____ First Europeans to reach North America

22. _____ First man to sail around Africa to India

23. _____ Built a sailing school in Portugal and planned trips around Africa to the Far East

24. _____ Probes that went to Jupiter, Saturn, Uranus, and Neptune

25. _____ American space station

26. _____ Space program that landed men on the moon

27. _____ Diving ship used to explore the deep ocean

28. _____ Russian space station

29. _____ Reusable American space ship

30. _____ Led the first voyage that successfully sailed around the world

31. _____ Probes that landed on Mars

32. _____ First American space program, ship held only one man

33. _____ First man made object put into space

34. _____ Second American space program, ship held two men

35. _____ He made two mistakes: thought the world was smaller than it is and did not know that the Americas blocked the route west from Europe to the Spice Islands

Answer the questions (4 points each answer).

36. Why were spices so expensive in Europe before the Age of Exploration?

_____

_____

_____

37. What does an aqualung do?

_____

_____

_____

38. Put north, south, east, and west in the correct place as they belong on a map.

a. _____

b. _____   d. _____

c. _____

39. Complete these sentences using the correct geography term.

a. A large body of salt water, often a part of the ocean surrounded by land or islands

is called a _____ .

b. An _____ is a narrow bridge of land connecting two larger pieces of land.

c. A _____ is a narrow waterway that connects two larger bodies of water.

d. A _____ is a piece of land almost surrounded by water or extending far

out into the water.

40. What did Europeans learn about the earth during the Age of Exploration?

_____

_____

_____

Write *true* or *false* on the line (2 points each answer).

41. _____ Three-fourths of the earth is covered with land.

42. _____ A globe is the best map of the earth.

43. _____ Neil Armstrong was the first person ever to orbit the earth.

44. _____ Lakes and rivers usually have salt water.

45. _____ Soviet/Russian space ships are manned by cosmonauts.

HISTORY & GEOGRAPHY 402

Unit 2: Seaport Cities

TEACHER NOTES

MATERIALS NEEDED FOR LIFEPAC	
Required	Suggested
• dictionary • encyclopedia • atlas, maps, globe • crayons, colored pencils or markers (the reference materials can be either in book or online formats)	• folk song, "My Darling Clementine" • pictures of the Australian flag

ADDITIONAL LEARNING ACTIVITIES

Section 1: Sydney, The Greatest Down-Under Seaport

1. Make a big seven-pointed star to represent the stars in the Australian flag and the seven divisions of Australia.

2. Draw a picture in two parts—Christmas in Sydney and Christmas in London—to depict the seasonal opposites.

3. Prepare a report on one of the two famous landmarks located in Sydney.

Section 2: Hong Kong, Marketplace of Asia

1. Collect clothing labels that read, "Made in Hong Kong."

2. Grow herbs (parsley, chives, etc.) in cans (allow for drainage).

3. Discuss how political changes have affected everyday life in Hong Kong.

Section 3: Istanbul

1. Obtain brochures, pictures and posters from travel bureaus and make your own posters.

2. Discuss the term East meets West.

3. Have the students give a report on a day of shopping in Istanbul. What items would they find? Describe the scene of an outdoor market.

Section 4: London

1. Sing British songs. A book of folk songs would help the students get the "feeling" of London. Songs such as: "God Save the Queen," "Sweet and Low," and "I've Got Sixpence, Jolly, Jolly, Sixpence."

2. Read poems and stories by English writers or about London—*Mary Poppins*, *Sing a Song of Sixpence*.

3. Invite a speaker from the Salvation Army to come and explain the Christian work they do there.

4. Write to the British Tourist Authority, or find their Internet site, for materials on London. They will send you a street map of Greater London for the asking. Travel bureaus also will supply you with materials on London.

5. Find and bring to class a clock with the Westminster four chimes. Also bring in a Big Ben alarm clock.

6. Write a report on John Wesley and the great revival that happened under his preaching.

7. Draw a picture in four parts. Show an activity that would be occurring in each of the four cities studied and at what time of day it would be in that city. For example: Istanbul, 7:00 P.M., someone going to a concert; London, 5:00 P.M., boat riding on the Thames or selling fish at Billingsgate; Hong Kong, 1:00 A.M., everyone in bed in a house-boat; Sydney, 3:00 A.M., a koala asleep in a eucalyptus tree.

8. Write a letter to the Chamber of Commerce, Lake Havasu City, Arizona, or visit their website for a picture of the London Bridge.

ADDITIONAL INFORMATION

Hong Kong is in the tropics. It lies between the two Tropic lines on the globe. The climate is warm which makes outdoor living and boat living comfortable. Crops can be raised throughout the year.

Istanbul is located in both Asia and Europe. It is the only major city in the world located on two continents. The climate is moderate. The temperatures can drop below zero.

London's grandeur is in her magnificent, old buildings; her meadow-like parks that brighten the dingy city; and the pageantry of the royal traditions—the gilded coach drawn by six white horses, the costumed guards on foot and on horseback, and the salute to the queen each year in the "Trooping the Colour" ceremony.

Queen Elizabeth inherited the throne from her father, King George V. Her husband is not a king, but prince Philip. They have four children, Prince Charles (born in 1948), Princes Anne (born in 1950), Prince Andrew (born in 1960), and Prince Edward (born in 1964). The family has homes in other parts of the country. Windsor Castle is upstream on the Thames River.

The Queen of England is also head of the Church of England. The kings and queens are crowned in front of the altar in Westminster Abbey. Behind the altar is a mosaic of the Last Supper. Above it are printed in English these words: "THE KINGDOMS OF OUR WORLD HAVE BECOME THE KINGDOMS OF OUR LORD AND OF HIS CHRIST."

London has considerable fog and rain. The warm Gulf Stream current moves along the shores of England and sends warm breezes across the land. When the warm ocean air meets the colder land air, fog and rain result. That is why Londoners always carry an umbrella.

Ford Motor Company's British plant is in London. British-made Jaguar, Triumph, MG, and Rolls Royce have offices in London. London is the business center of all British industry. Many products are sent to London for export via the Thames River.

Most important of all, the roots of the United States are in Britain and in her greatest city, London.

ADDITIONAL ACTIVITIES

This additional activity sheet may be copied and handed out to the students. All students will enjoy coloring the Tower of London and the Beefeater. Try to make a picture of Beefeaters available so the student can color his picture accurately to learn how one looks.

The questions serve as a review of the facts about the Tower. Students may enjoy finding out more about the Tower of London and the Beefeaters. They could work together on these questions.

TEACHERS ANSWER KEY (ACTIVITY ON NEXT PAGE)

The first tower was built by _King William I_ as a lookout tower to guard _London_. Later, other towers were added. The tower was once used as a _prison_. Now the tower is a _museum_. The warders of the tower are called _beefeaters_. The _jewels_ of the kings and queens are kept in the Tower of London.

Administer the LIFEPAC Test.

> The test is to be administered in one session. Give no help except with directions.
> Evaluate the tests and review areas where the students have done poorly.
> Review the pages and activities that stress the concepts tested.
> If necessary, administer the Alternate LIFEPAC Test.

Color the picture and complete the statement. Turn back to the LIFEPAC if you cannot remember the answers.

The first tower was built by _____ as a lookout tower to guard _____ .

Later, other towers were added. The tower was once used as a _____ . Now the tower

is a _____ . The warders of the tower are called _____ . The

_____ of the kings and queens are kept in the Tower of London.

ANSWER KEYS

SECTION 1

1.1-1.4 Teacher check
1.5 west
1.6 harbor
1.7 penal colony
1.8 First Fleet
1.9 Captain James Cook
1.10 Port Jackson
1.11 animals ran away, people did not have the right skills, supplies came late, crops did not grow
1.12 New South Wales, because it reminded him of his home
1.13 They could not afford to pay for a return trip.
1.14 Gold
1.15 sheep
1.16 1842
1.17 Commonwealth of Australia
1.18 Teacher check
1.19 Any order:
   a. Opera House
   b. Sydney Harbour Bridge
1.20 21
1.21 coat hanger
1.22 Sydney lace
1.23 true
1.24 true
1.25 false
1.26 true
1.27 b
1.28 c
1.29 e
1.30 a
1.31 d
1.32 false
1.33 true
1.34 false
1.35 false
1.36 true
1.37 Teacher check
1.38 true
1.39 true
1.40 false
1.41 false
1.42 Any three: tea, cricket, rugby, soccer, drive on left side of the road
1.43 Teacher check

SELF TEST 1

1.01 j
1.02 c
1.03 g
1.04 b
1.05 f
1.06 a
1.07 e
1.08 d
1.09 h
1.010 i
1.011 b
1.012 h
1.013 a
1.014 j
1.015 g
1.016 e
1.017 f
1.018 i
1.019 c
1.020 d
1.021 true
1.022 true
1.023 true
1.024 true
1.025 true
1.026 false
1.027 false
1.028 true
1.029 They could not afford to pay for passage home.
1.030 Sydney's winter and summer are the opposite of ours because they are south of the equator and we are north of it.
1.031 Any two: bushwalking, going to the beach, or yachting
1.032 Australia became independent gradually, without a war.
1.033 penal
1.034 peninsula
1.035 sheep
1.036 gold
1.037 ferry
1.038 nets

SECTION 2

2.1	Teacher check
2.2	Opium
2.3	Britain
2.4	opium
2.5	Any order: Hong Kong Island, Kowloon, New Territories
2.6	false
2.7	true
2.8	true
2.9	false
2.10	false
2.11	true
2.13	c
2.14	e
2.15	b
2.16	a
2.17	d
2.18	polluted
2.19	British
2.20	Any order:

a. make more land in the ocean
b. live on boats
c. dig out places on the mountains
d. tear down old buildings and build bigger new ones

2.21	Any order: hard work, food
2.22	Chinese New Year
2.23	Bun Festival
2.24	mah-jong
2.25	fresh
2.26	Chinese Opera
2.27	Any order: shopping, food
2.28	large fields (open areas)
2.29	eight
2.30	Any order:

a. Confucianism
b. Taoism
c. Buddhism

2.31	*feng shui* man
2.32	Confucius
2.33	good luck

SELF TEST 2

2.01	farms
2.02	boats
2.03	opium
2.04	99
2.05	refugees
2.06	hard work (or food)
2.07	penal
2.08	Chinese New Year
2.09	British
2.010	south
2.011	false
2.012	false
2.013	false
2.014	true
2.015	true
2.016	true
2.017	false
2.018	true
2.019	false
2.020	false
2.021	d
2.022	f
2.023	b
2.024	i
2.025	e
2.026	a
2.027	g
2.028	h
2.029	j
2.030	c
2.031	Teacher check: Answers include - Sydney is spread out, Hong Kong is crowded; Sydneysiders like outdoor sports, Hong Kong people work hard; Sydney's people came from Britain, Hong Kong's from China
2.032	People are willing to work cheaply; and it is a duty free port.
2.033	People like to visit Hong Kong for the shopping and the food.
2.034	winter
2.035	lace
2.036	Sea
2.037	Pacific
2.038	Asia

SECTION 3

3.1	Teacher check
3.2	Byzantium
3.3	Byzantine
3.4	Constantine
3.5	Constantinople
3.6	1,000
3.7	Rome, Constantinople
3.8	b
3.9	a
3.10	c
3.11	d
3.12	true
3.13	true
3.14	false
3.15	false
3.16	a. Byzantium, Greeks
	b. Constantinople, Romans or Byzantine
	c. Istanbul, Ottoman Turks
3.17	false
3.18	true
3.19	false
3.20	false
3.21	false
3.22-3.24	Teacher check
3.25	mosque
3.26	Topkapi
3.27	water
3.28	Suleiman the Magnificent
3.29	Hippodrome
3.30	Hagia Sophia
3.31	Justinian I
3.32	c
3.33	d
3.34	a
3.35	f
3.36	b
3.37	e
3.38	dolma
3.39	works
3.40	rules
3.41	baklava
3.42	Romans
3.43	buses, ferries, or dolmus
3.44	Grand Bazaar
3.45	talk, play backgammon, smoke a hookah

SELF TEST 3

3.01	Byzantium
3.02	Constantinople
3.03	Ottoman Turks (or Mehmet II).
3.04	Australia
3.05	World War I
3.06	church
3.07	Grand Bazaar
3.08	Chinese
3.09	Pacific
3.010	Suez
3.011	Africa
3.012	a peninsula
3.013	northern
3.014	sheep
3.015	an archipelago
3.016	Sea
3.017	Sydney
3.018	Africa
3.019	good luck
3.020	Indian
3.021	j
3.022	d
3.023	h
3.024	k
3.025	b
3.026	i
3.027	l
3.028	c
3.029	a
3.030	g
3.031	f
3.032	e
3.033	true
3.034	true
3.035	false
3.036	true
3.037	false
3.038	true
3.039	true
3.040	true
3.041	false
3.042	false
3.043	true
3.044	Chinese religion is a mix of Confucianism, Taoism, and Buddhism. People believe mostly in good or bad luck and use fortune tellers (*feng shui* men) to find it.
3.045	The religion of Istanbul is Islam, which believes in one god, salvation by works following strict rules.

3.046 Istanbul is on two peninsulas across the Bosporus from each other. One is in Europe. The other is in Asia. The Black Sea is to the north and the Sea of Marmara is to the south.

SECTION 4

4.1 Londinium

4.2 A.D. 43

4.3 Westminster Abbey

4.4 a. White Tower
 b. William the Conqueror

4.5 Saxons

4.6 Any order:
 a. England
 b. Scotland
 c. Wales
 d. Northern Ireland

4.7 Any order:
 a. Black Death (Bubonic Plague)
 b. Great Fire

4.8 London Bridge

4.9 St. Paul's

4.10 Westminster

4.11 British

4.12 London Blitz

4.13 Winston Churchill

4.14 The British Empire was so large, all over the world, that it was always daytime somewhere in the empire.

4.15 Constantine also built the city of Constantinople that is now Istanbul. The first Hagia Sophia was also built by Constantine

4.16 e

4.17 d

4.18 b

4.19 a

4.20 c

4.21 true

4.22 false

4.23 true

4.24 true

4.25 true

4.26 false

4.27 dome

4.28 Westminster

4.29 Admiral Nelson

4.30 Buckingham Palace

4.31 British Museum

4.32 Great Fire

4.33 Number 10, Downing Street

4.34 Any order:
 a. Magna Carta
 b. a Gutenberg Bible

4.35 Big Ben

4.36 Any order:
 a. House of Commons
 b. House of Lords

4.37 c

4.38	b
4.39	d
4.40	e
4.41	a
4.42	The House of Commons shows it is independent of the queen by not answering the door on the first knock.
4.43	The Colour is the flag of a regiment.
4.44	g
4.45	e
4.46	c
4.47	a
4.48	b
4.49	d
4.50	f
4.51	true
4.52	false
4.53	false
4.54	true
4.55	The people of Sydney go to the Anglican Church because they came from Britain and that is the British government church.
4.56	Big Ben
4.57	Westminster
4.58	City
4.59	parliament
4.60	Wren
4.61	Romans
4.62	Abbey
4.63	Thames
4.64	William
4.65	Buckingham
4.66	bank

SELF TEST 4

4.01	the City
4.02	Tower of London
4.03	Hong Kong
4.04	Romans
4.05	London Bridge
4.06	Sydney
4.07	Great Fire
4.08	British Empire
4.09	London Blitz
4.010	h
4.011	g
4.012	a
4.013	e
4.014	c
4.015	d
4.016	f
4.017	b
4.018	true
4.019	false
4.020	true
4.021	true
4.022	false
4.023	false
4.024	false
4.025	false
4.026	true
4.027	false
4.028	true
4.029	true
4.030	London
4.031	Hong Kong
4.032	Sydney
4.033	London
4.034	Istanbul
4.035	Differences: Chinese vs. British people; Chinese religion vs. Anglican Church; spread out vs. crowded; and any others the student may find
4.036	both harbor cities, ruled by Romans, many old buildings and royal palaces

LIFEPAC TEST

1. Sydney
2. Istanbul
3. Istanbul
4. London
5. Hong Kong
6. Sydney
7. London
8. Istanbul
9. Hong Kong
10. Hong Kong
11. continent
12. Sea
13. archipelago
14. Island
15. Isthmus
16. strait
17. mouth
18. harbor
19. peninsula
20. Ocean
21. b
22. g
23. h
24. i
25. d
26. a
27. e
28. j
29. c
30. f
31. sheep
32. Constantinople
33. the City
34. Sydneysiders
35. Cockney
36. hard work (or food)
37. opium
38. (either order) Lords, Commons
39. Tower of London
40. Britain
41. true
42. false
43. false
44. true
45. true
46. true
47. false
48. true
49. true
50. false

ALTERNATE LIFEPAC TEST

1. d
2. a
3. e
4. f
5. g
6. c
7. b
8. i
9. h
10. e
11. g
12. a
13. b
14. c
15. d
16. f
17. S
18. HK
19. L
20. I
21. Constantinople
22. Great Fire
23. Buckingham Palace
24. Big Ben
25. Chinese New Year
26. Ramadan
27. opium
28. strait
29. Isthmus
30. true
31. true
32. false
33. false
34. true
35. false
36. Examples:
   Both are port cities with fine harbors. They are ancient cities once ruled by the Romans. They have many old buildings, churches, and royal palaces.

HISTORY & GEOGRAPHY 402

ALTERNATE LIFEPAC TEST

NAME _____

DATE _____

SCORE _____

80

100

Match these items (3 points each answer).

1. _____ James Cook
2. _____ Winston Churchill
3. _____ Christopher Wren
4. _____ Lord Nelson
5. _____ Confucius
6. _____ *Feng shui* man
7. _____ Constantine

a. the Prime Minister of Great Britain during World War II

b. first Christian Roman Emperor

c. Chinese fortune teller

d. he named Australia New South Wales

e. a great architect

f. a great hero of the British navy

g. most Chinese people follow his teachings

Match these items (3 points each answer).

8. _____ Home of the House of Commons
9. _____ the smallest continent
10. _____ a building that looks like a sailing ship
11. _____ church where British rulers are crowned
12. _____ "The Old Lady of Threadneedle Street"
13. _____ Victoria, Kowloon, and New Territories
14. _____ City in Asia and Europe
15. _____ Golden Gate Bridge crosses the harbor mouth
16. _____ Byzantine church

a. the Bank of England

b. Hong Kong

c. Istanbul

d. San Francisco

e. Sydney's Opera House

f. Hagia Sophia

g. Westminster Abbey

h. Australia

i. London

Write which seaport city is indicated. Use *I* for Istanbul, *S* for Sydney, *HK* for Hong Kong, and *L* for London (2 points each answer).

17. _____ a colony for prisoners

18. _____ a home for Chinese refugees

19. _____ started by the Romans

20. _____ started by the Greeks

Fill in the blanks with words from this list (3 points each answer).

Big Ben	Constantinople	Ramadan
strait	Buckingham Palace	Isthmus
Chinese New Year	opium	Great Fire

21. Istanbul was called _____ by the Byzantines.

22. London was almost destroyed in A.D. 1666 by the _____ .

23. The Queen's London home is _____ .

24. The clock in the tower at London's Parliament is called _____ .

25. The biggest holiday in Hong Kong is _____ .

26. _____ is the Muslim month of fasting.

27. The British forced the Chinese to trade _____ for tea and silk.

28. The English Channel is a _____ between Britain and Europe.

29. North and South America are connected by the _____ of Panama.

Write *true* or *false* on the line (2 points each answer).

30. _____ Sydney has summer when San Francisco has winter.

31. _____ A harbor is a bay deep enough to shelter ships.

32. _____ Muslims believe in salvation by grace (belief in Jesus).

33. _____ Sydney is one of the world's most crowded cities.

34. _____ The palaces of the Ottoman sultan are in Istanbul.

35. _____ Hong Kong people are famous for being lazy.

Answer this question (5 points).

36.   How are London and Istanbul alike?

_____

_____

_____

_____

_____

HISTORY & GEOGRAPHY 403

Unit 3: Desert Lands

TEACHER NOTES

MATERIALS NEEDED FOR LIFEPAC	
Required	Suggested
• dictionary • encyclopedia • atlas, maps, globe • crayons, colored pencils or markers (the reference materials can be either in book or online formats)	• pictures of desert plants • pictures of camels and palm trees • long grass (plastic, yarn, or jute) for braiding mats • map of Africa • pictures of nomads and their tents • picture of the tabernacle of Moses • map of Australia • pictures of kangaroos, koalas, eucalyptus trees, kookaburra, and emu birds • a boomerang • encyclopedia or books about Australian animals • map of Southwest United States • pictures of Native Americans (Navajos and Hopis) • pictures of Arizona canals for irrigation • pictures of the Painted Desert and Monument Valley • pictures of pueblos

ADDITIONAL LEARNING ACTIVITIES

Section 1: What is a Desert

1. Conduct map drills.

2. Collect pictures of desert animals and plants and display them.

3. Have a date and coconut tasting party.

4. Draw and color a world map labeling the large desert areas.

Section 2: Where are the Deserts

1. Videos on the Sahara Desert may be available online.

2. Collect pictures of nomad dress, tents, and camels and make a display.

3. Use five yards of cloth and wrap a boy's head to show the nomad headdress and veil.

4. Use different materials (strips of construction paper, plastic rope, jute, etc.) and braid or weave mats.

5. Draw and color a nomad tent, nomads, or a camel caravan.

6. Write a report on mining salt in the Sahara, desert sandstorms, the Muslim religion, or related topics.

Section 3: How do People Live in the Deserts

1. Conduct map drills.

2. Videos on the Arabian desert and oil production available through educational division of major oil companies.

3. Invite a missionary or tourist from Arabia, Australia, or the Native Americans to come and share with the class.

4. Read Isaiah 35:1 through 7. Discuss how this can happen and is happening in Israel today. Also relate the verses to our own spiritual experience of how the Holy Spirit can turn trials into rich experiments that become real blessings.

5. Make a bulletin board display of the deserts of the world. A large world map can be made by each group, making a different continent and shading the desert areas. Obtain or draw pictures of the people, plants, animals, or unique features of each desert area and apply to the map.

6. Sing the "Kookaburra" round. This Australian folk song about the kookaburra can be sung as a round. Use three groups.

Kookaburra sits on an old gum tree,
Merry, merry king of the bush is he,
Laugh, kookaburra, laugh, kookaburra,
Gay your life must be.

Kookaburra sits on the old gum tree,
Eating all the gum drops he can see.
Stop, Kookaburra! Stop, Kookaburra!
Leave some there for me.

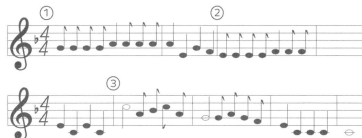

7. Write reports on Australian animals, an oasis, Hopi or Navaho art, or oil drilling in Arabia.

8. Tell briefly the story around the Bible characters who lived in the Arabian desert (Moses and the children of Israel, Jesus and his desert experience, John the Baptist, etc).

ADDITIONAL ACTIVITY

The picture may be colored as an extra activity. The questions may be answered independently or completed by groups depending on the availability of reference books, time, and student ability. Gifted students could write a short report comparing and contrasting dromedaries and camels.

TEACHER'S ANSWER KEY FOR *SHIPS OF THE SAHARA*

1. A dromedary is a one-humped camel.

2. Dromedaries are used for riding and can travel up to one hundred miles a day.

3. Camels are used most often to carry heavy loads from one place to another.

4. Camels' eyes are naturally protected from blowing sand by two rows of eyelashes instead of one. They can completely close their nostrils for protection from blowing sand during sandstorms.

5. Most adult camels can carry up to four hundred pounds.

6. Camels store water in their tissues and use it from their tissues rather than from the blood. A camel can lose water equal to 25 percent of his body weight with no signs of distress whereas man is in dire distress after a 21 percent loss. Camels can drink about twenty-ty-seven gallons of water in ten minutes.

Administer the LIFEPAC Test.

> The test is to be administered in one session. Give no help except with directions.
> Evaluate the tests and review areas where the students have done poorly.
> Review the pages and activities that stress the concepts tested.
> If necessary, administer the Alternate LIFEPAC Test.

ANSWER KEYS

SECTION 1

1.1	south
1.2	west
1.3	north
1.4	east
1.5	south
1.6	east
1.7	Cancer; Capricorn
1.8	10
1.9	rocks
1.10	rain shadow
1.11	food or water
1.12	blanket
1.13	d
1.14	b
1.15	c
1.16	a
1.17	(any four) waxy coating, sponge-like inside, deep roots, spread out roots, leaves that collect fog or dew, grow quickly after a rain
1.18	c
1.19	d
1.20	e
1.21	a
1.22	b
1.23	f
1.24	(any four) wide hoof, small slit at nose, extra eyelid, hair in ears, store fat in hump, store water in stomach, get moisture from food; not sweat much; can carry 400 pounds
1.25	Teacher check

SELF TEST 1

1.01	false
1.02	true
1.03	false
1.04	true
1.05	true
1.06	false
1.07	false
1.08	true
1.09	false
1.010	true
1.011	c
1.012	f
1.013	g
1.014	j
1.015	b
1.016	i
1.017	e
1.018	h
1.019	a
1.020	d
1.021	Cancer
1.022	Capricorn
1.023	(any order) saguaro, prickly pear
1.024	blanket
1.025	equator
1.026	rocks
1.027	fog
1.028	moisture
1.029	roots
1.030	The clouds cool as they go up the mountain and lose their moisture. The side without moisture is the rain shadow.
1.031	Any three: wide hoof, small slit at nose, extra eyelid, hair in ears, store fat in hump, store water in stomach, get moisture from food; not sweat much; can carry 400 pounds
1.032	A dry area that usually receives 10 inches of rain or less in a year
1.033	Any three: plants, seeds, insects, other animals

SECTION 2

2.1	American Southwest
2.2	Atacama
2.3	(either order)
	a. Sahara
	b. Kalahari
2.4	(either order)
	a. Arabian
	b. Gobi
2.5	Australian
2.6	none
2.7	oil
2.8	Sahel
2.9	Atlas
2.10	wadis
2.11	Rub´ al-Khali
2.12	Cancer
2.13	Sahara
2.14	Nile
2.15	Rockies; Sierra Madres; Andes
2.16	Death Valley
2.17	*steppes*
2.18	Thar
2.19	Mongolia
2.20	false
2.21	true
2.22	true
2.23	false
2.24	true

2.25	false
2.26	true
2.27	Pica
2.28	*playa*
2.29	Andes
2.30	hemisphere
2.31	Patagonian
2.32	Australian
2.33	*salars*
2.34	pans
2.35	Cold water from Antarctica makes the air along the coast cold, and it loses its moisture.
2.36	There is very little water on top of the ground.

CROSSWORD REVIEW

2.37

Across	Down
3. Great basin	1. Death Valley
5. Thar	2. Sahara
6. American	4. Cancer
8. Arabian	6. Atacama
10. Australian	7. Patagonian
11. Atlas	9. Kalahari
14. Capricorn	12. Namib
15. Rub´ al-Khali	13. Nile
16. Gobi	

SELF TEST 2

2.01	true
2.02	true
2.03	true
2.04	false
2.05	false
2.06	false
2.07	false
2.08	true
2.09	true
2.010	true
2.011	true
2.012	Tropic of Capricorn
2.013	Tropic of Cancer
2.014	Northern Hemisphere
2.015	Southern Hemisphere
2.016	f
2.017	h
2.018	d
2.019	j
2.020	i
2.021	c
2.022	a
2.023	e
2.024	g
2.025	b
2.026	Atacama
2.027	Sahara
2.028	Gobi
2.029	American Southwest
2.030	Arabian
2.031	Australian
2.032	Kalahari

2.033-2.037 (partial credit can be given)

2.033 The side away from water where the moisture can not reach. It is lost as the cloud cools going over the mountain.

2.034 The cold water from Antarctica makes the air along the coast cold and it loses its moisture.

2.035 The water in them can not get out; it evaporates and leaves salt behind.

2.036 Any three:
wide hoof, small slit at nose, extra eyelid, hair in ears, stores fat in hump, stores water in stomach, gets moisture from food; does not sweat much; can carry 400 pounds

2.037 It keeps out the heat of the sun during the day and keeps heat in at night.

SECTION 3

3.1	very little
3.2	men; women
3.3	Any order:
	a. hunter/gathers
	b. nomads
	c. villagers
3.4	home
3.5	desert
3.6	possessions
3.7	salt
3.8	animals
3.9	horses
3.10	Any order: meat, milk, skins
3.11	They moved to find food for their animals.
3.12	Any order: trade, use of oasis, insults
3.13	f
3.14	b
3.15	e
3.16	d
3.17	a
3.18	c
3.19	Teacher check
3.20	false
3.21	true
3.22	true
3.23	false
3.24	true
3.25	true
3.26	Any order:
	a. build a canal
	b. dam a river
	c. dig a well
3.27	irrigation
3.28	hydroponics
3.29	Phoenix, Arizona
3.30	a. keep people cool inside
	b. allows quick travel/ bring in food
3.31	sunlight
3.32	They put up plastic sheets or nets to catch water from the fog.
3.33	underground
3.34	sunlight
3.35	hard
3.36	water
3.37	radio
3.38	light colors
3.39	Teacher check

SELF TEST 3

3.01   p
3.02   d
3.03   g
3.04   a
3.05   k
3.06   b
3.07   l
3.08   n
3.09   o
3.010 m
3.011 c
3.012 e
3.013 f
3.014 h
3.015 i
3.016 j
3.017 Africa
3.018 South America
3.019 North America
3.020 Africa
3.021 Asia
3.022 Asia
3.023 Australia
3.024 Cancer
3.025 Capricorn
3.026 Mongol
3.027 Berber
3.028 hemisphere
3.029 pueblos
3.030 They put up plastic sheets or nets to catch moisture from the fog.
3.031 Either order:
   a. by mountains (in the rain shadow)
   b. by cold water from Antarctica
3.032 The water can not get out; it evaporates and leaves salt behind.
3.033 true
3.034 false
3.035 true
3.036 true
3.037 true
3.038 false
3.039 false
3.040 true
3.041 true

LIFEPAC TEST

1. true
2. true
3. false
4. false
5. true
6. false
7. false
8. false
9. true
10. true
11. false
12. Tropic of Capricorn
13. Tropic of Cancer
14. salt
15. horse
16. Northern Hemisphere
17. Any one: dig a well, build a canal, dam a river
18. Sahara
19. oil
20. Southern Hemisphere
21. hunter/gatherers
22. at night
23. e
24. c
25. f
26. h
27. j
28. k
29. b
30. d
31. a
32. g
33. i
34. l
35. North America
36. South America
37. Africa
38. Africa
39. Asia
40. Asia
41. Australia
42. Europe
43. They use plastic sheets or nets to collect water from the fog.
44. Either order:
    a. by mountains (the desert is in the mountain's rain shadow)
    b. by cold Antarctic water

ALTERNATE LIFEPAC TEST

1. Europe
2. American Southwest
3. Atacama
4. Arabian
5. Gobi
6. Kalahari
7. Sahara
8. Australian
9. Either order:
    a. Northern Hemisphere
    b. Southern Hemisphere
10. Either order:
    a. Tropic of Cancer
    b. Tropic of Capricorn
11. 10
12. rain shadow
13. Antarctica
14. Sahara
15. false
16. true
17. true
18. false
19. false
20. true
21. false
22. true
23. j
24. a
25. b
26. h
27. i
28. d
29. e
30. c
31. g
32. f
33. Any order:
    dig a well, build a canal, dam a river
34. Any three:
    spread out roots, deep roots, sponge-like insides, waxy coating, grow quickly after a rain, leaves that collect fog or dew
35. Any two:
    insects, seeds, plants, other animals

HISTORY & GEOGRAPHY 403

ALTERNATE LIFEPAC TEST

NAME _____

DATE _____

SCORE _____

80

100

Put the correct word in the blank (3 points each answer).

American Southwest	Sahara	Kalahari
Atacama	Arabian	Gobi
Australian	Europe	

1. The are no deserts on the continent of _____ .

2. The _____ Desert is partly in Mexico.

3. The _____ Desert is in South America.

4. The _____ Desert is in southwest Asia.

5. The _____ Desert is in Mongolia, Asia.

6. The _____ Desert is in Botswana in southern Africa.

7. The _____ Desert is in North Africa.

8. The _____ Desert is on a continent that is also a country.

Complete these sentences (4 points each answer).

9. The equator divides the earth into two halves:

   a. _____ and

   b. _____ .

10. The two imaginary lines of dry area that circle the earth are:

    a. _____ and

    b. _____ .

11. A desert usually has _____ or less inches of rain in a year.

12. A desert forms in the _____ of a mountain that blocks its moisture.

13. Deserts have formed on the coast when the cold current along it has come from _____ _____ .

14. The largest desert in the world is the _____ .

Answer _true_ or _false_ (1 point each answer).

15. _____ Desert plants die when it rains.

16. _____ The people of the Atacama get water from the fog by using plastic sheets or nets.

17. _____ Desert animals often live in burrows during the day and hunt for food at night.

18. _____ Death Valley is the highest place in Africa.

19. _____ The Atlas Mountains are in North America.

20. _____ Deserts are often covered with sand or rocks.

21. _____ Hunter/gatherers carried many possessions with them.

22. _____ The Nile River is in the Sahara Desert.

Match the following (2 points each answer).

23. _____ nomad

24. _____ hunter/gatherers

25. _____ horses

26. _____ camels

27. _____ pueblo

28. _____ Sahel

29. _____ oil

30. _____ solar panel

31. _____ salt

32. _____ _steppes_

a. people who kill and find food

b. Mongol's most important animal

c. makes electricity from sunlight

d. area south of the Sahara

e. Arabian Desert is rich in this

f. flat grassland of the Gobi

g. caravans traded it across the Sahara

h. "ship of the desert"

i. Hopi village

j. people who move to find food for their animals

Answer the questions (2 points each answer).

33. List three modern ways to bring water into a desert.

    a. _____

    b. _____

    c. _____

34. List three ways God made plants special in order to live in the desert.

    a. _____

    b. _____

    c. _____

35. List two things animals can eat in the desert.

    a. _____

    b. _____

HISTORY & GEOGRAPHY 404

Unit 4: Grasslands

TEACHER NOTES

MATERIALS NEEDED FOR LIFEPAC	
Required	Suggested
• dictionary • encyclopedia • atlas, maps, globe • crayons, colored pencils or markers (the reference materials can be either in book or online formats)	• samples of different kinds of grasses • a few boxes of common cereals or foods containing grass plants—grains (labels will show this)

ADDITIONAL LEARNING ACTIVITIES

Section 1: Ukraine

1. Attitudes and appreciations to develop.

    a. Help students realize the importance of grass plants in our everyday life.

    b. Be sure students realize the variety of places or locations where grasslands are to be found.

2. Discuss these questions with your class.

    a. How did people first realize the importance of grass foods?

    b. Where do grasses grow?

    c. How do we use grass plants today?

    d. What do we mean by "dry" farms?

    e. What is usually raised on "dry" farms?

    f. What is a ranch?

    g. What do we mean by tropical grasslands?

    h. How does rainfall affect the type of grass grown in an area?

3. Bread is considered to be the "Staff of Life." Why? Bread is made from flour. Flour is ground from grain—a grass plant. If possible show student how wheat is separated from chaff. Use rocks to show how wheat was ground long ago. If at all possible make bread in class. If demonstration is not possible, go through the process orally.

4. Set up a display table labeled "Grass Foods." Bring in boxes with labels showing the ingredients from grass plants.

5. Visit a bakery where bread is made on a large scale.

6. Visit any manufacturing company in your area that uses any form of grass plants.

7. Look up information on Arbor Day. Where did it begin? How did it begin? Why did it begin? Is it still celebrated? Write or give an oral report on Arbor Day.

8. Keep a diary for a day. How many grass foods did you eat?

9. Jesus said, "I am the bread of life." Make a poster or motto using this idea.

10. Ask your teacher or parents to help you find a story mentioned in the Bible where a grass food is mentioned. Tell the story to your class.

11. Discuss the old and new aspects of Ukraine.

Section 2: Kenya

1. Discuss these questions with your class.

    a. What kind of grasslands are in Kenya?

    b. What do Europeans do in Kenya? (farm and missions)

    c. Find a grassland city in Kenya. (Nairobi)

2. Draw maps of the continents with grasslands and color the grassland areas green and the rest of the area another color. Use a map key.

Section 3: Argentina

1. Discuss these questions with your class.

    a. Describe an Argentina "estancia."

    b. Describe an Argentine "gaucho."

    c. What do gauchos do today?

    d. What does a gaucho look like?

    e. How is meat shipped to Europe from Argentina?

    f. Describe the Argentina "Pampas."

    g. Why is meat sent to Europe?

2. Choose a grassland animal and write a report on its life cycle, its nesting habits, or eating habits. Tell if it is a predator and what animal it preys upon and what animals it is prey for.

3. Write and illustrate a report on an Argentina ranch.

ADDITIONAL ACTIVITY

An extra activity is given for the student who needs clarification on the four kinds of grass regions and where each kind grows. This could also be used as a fun activity by those who enjoy drawing. Students could work together on this activity and make the drawing large enough for display.

Administer the LIFEPAC Test.

> The test is to be administered in one session. Give no help except with directions.
> Evaluate the tests and review areas where the students have done poorly.
> Review the pages and activities that stress the concepts tested.
> If necessary, administer the Alternate LIFEPAC Test.

STUDENT INSTRUCTIONS

Draw a picture in four parts. Draw and color grass as it grows in each of the four kinds of areas. Include something from the area—mountains, an animal, or grain. Label each part of your picture: steppes, prairies, savannas, and alpine.

ANSWER KEYS

SECTION 1

1.1	Africa	**1.32**	circle: uranium, iron ore, nickel, manganese, titanium
1.2	South America		
1.3	North America	**1.33**	8
1.4	savanna	**1.34**	4
1.5	prairie	**1.35**	1
1.6	steppe	**1.36**	3
1.7	grass	**1.37**	5
1.8	true	**1.38**	2
1.9	false	**1.39**	6
1.10	true	**1.40**	7
1.11	true	**1.41**	true
1.12	false	**1.42**	true
1.13	true	**1.43**	true
1.14	false	**1.44**	false
1.15	true	**1.45**	false
1.16	false	**1.46**	true
1.17	true	**1.47**	false
1.18	bay or gulf	**1.48**	false
1.19	Russia	**1.49**	slavs
1.20	Any two: Poland, Slovakia, Hungary, Romania, Moldova	**1.50**	pysanky
		1.51	patriarchs
1.21	Crimea	**1.52**	bandura
1.22	Sea of Azov and the Black Sea	**1.53**	Byzantine
1.23	Breadbasket of Europe	**1.54**	true
1.24	The Steppes	**1.55**	true
1.25	Carpathian and Crimean	**1.56**	true
1.26	Kiev	**1.57**	false
1.27	Dnepr	**1.58**	true
1.28	Crimea	**1.59**	false
1.29	Odessa		
1.30	chernozem		
1.31	sugar beets and wheat		

SELF TEST 1

1.01	chernozem
1.02	Pampas
1.03	communist
1.04	icon
1.05	steppe
1.06	pysanky
1.07	prairie
1.08	serf
1.09	savanna
1.010	collective
1.011	They are good place to grow crops because they are flat, fertile, and many food crops are grass.
1.012	The communist government took the food away and gave it to other parts of the USSR.
1.013	c
1.014	b
1.015	j
1.016	i
1.017	f
1.018	d
1.019	a
1.020	e
1.021	g
1.022	h
1.023	false
1.024	true
1.025	true
1.026	true
1.027	false
1.028	false
1.029	true
1.030	true
1.031	true
1.032	false

SECTION 2

2.1	north
2.2	Somalia
2.3	Lake Victoria
2.4	Mombasa or Malindi
2.5	Kere-Nyagah
2.6	Indian
2.7	Nairobi
2.8	Rift
2.9	Victoria
2.10	Turkana, Chalbi
2.11	false
2.12	true
2.13	true
2.14	false
2.15	true
2.16	false
2.17	Teacher check
2.18	Greeks, Romans, Arabs
2.19	Mombasa, Malindi
2.20	Swahili
2.21	about 100 years
2.22	Sultan of Oman
2.23	slave trade
2.24	The European countries divided it up among themselves without any Africans present.
2.25	2
2.26	4
2.27	5
2.28	3
2.29	6
2.30	1
2.31	7
2.32	The government forced them to sell their land or business to Black Kenyans.
2.33	gave them an education
2.34	It is the source of the Nile River
2.35	It took all of the land the Blacks were not using and gave all of the best land to the White settlers.
2.36	Teacher check. It the student says he does not have enough information, have him list the things he wants to know instead.
2.37	A piece of land that is a Kenyan's home among his tribe.
2.38	about 40
	Any two:
	Kikuyu, Kalenjin, Kamba, Luhya, Luo
2.39	f
2.40	d
2.41	a
2.42	b
2.43	e

2.44	c
2.45	true
2.46	false
2.47	true
2.48	false

SELF TEST 2

2.01	U
2.02	U
2.03	K
2.04	K
2.05	U
2.06	K
2.07	K
2.08	U
2.09	U
2.010	K
2.011	Nairobi
2.012	Mombasa
2.013	Crimea
2.014	Dnepr
2.015	Swahili
2.016	Uganda
2.017	Russia
2.018	Kiev
2.019	Cossacks
2.020	Chalbi
2.021	Mt. Kenya, tallest mountain in the country
2.022	It is the source of the Nile River.
2.023	to see the animals
2.024	slave trade
2.025	They are good for growing crops because they are flat, fertile, and many food crops are grass.
2.026	false
2.027	false
2.028	false
2.029	true
2.030	false
2.031	true
2.032	true
2.033	false
2.034	true
2.035	true

SECTION 3

3.1   d
3.2   k
3.3   e
3.4   a
3.5   h
3.6   j
3.7   f
3.8   i
3.9   b
3.10 c
3.11 g
3.12 They did not find gold and silver there.
3.13 1580
3.14 It was made the capital of a new colony, the Viceroyalty of La Plata.
3.15 Whether there would be a strong government in Buenos Aires or the provinces would control themselves.
3.16 He convinced the provinces to declare independence and defeated the Spanish.
3.17 A dictator who ruled from 1829-1853 and drove the Indians off the Pampas.
3.18 false
3.19 true
3.20 false
3.21 true
3.22 false
3.23 true
3.24 false
3.25 true
3.26 true
3.27 true
3.28 e
3.29 c
3.30 f
3.31 b
3.32 a
3.33 d
3.34 g
3.35 true
3.36 false
3.37 false
3.38 true
3.39 true
3.40 true

3.41   Word search puzzle key:

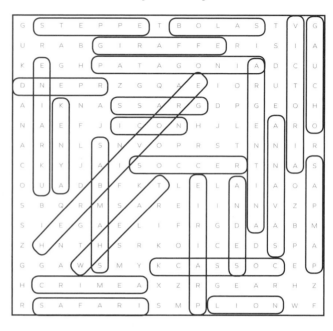

SELF TEST 3

3.01	K
3.02	U
3.03	K
3.04	K
3.05	U
3.06	A
3.07	A
3.08	K
3.09	U
3.010	U
3.011	j
3.012	i
3.013	h
3.014	a
3.015	b
3.016	c
3.017	g
3.018	d
3.019	e
3.020	f

3.021 Selling food raised on the Pampas to the industrial nations of Europe.

3.022 The communist government took away their crops and gave it to other parts of the USSR.

3.023 Inflation and debt

3.024 People come, pay to see the animals, and spend money in the country.

3.025 A cowboy of the Pampas

3.026	false
3.027	true
3.028	true
3.029	true
3.030	false
3.031	false
3.032	true
3.033	true
3.034	true
3.035	true
3.036	Buenos Aires
3.037	Cossacks
3.038	Swahili
3.039	Great Rift
3.040	equator
3.041	Tropic of Capricorn
3.042	Nairobi
3.043	Dnepr
3.044	Kiev
3.045	Chernobyl

LIFEPAC TEST

1.	U
2.	U
3.	U
4.	K
5.	K
6.	A
7.	K
8.	A
9.	A
10.	U
11.	K
12.	A
13.	K
14.	U
15.	A
16.	K
17.	A
18.	A
19.	K
20.	U
21.	Tierra del Fuego
22.	Black
23.	Crimea
24.	Nairobi
25.	Perón
26.	Carpathian
27.	Swahili
28.	Kiev
29.	Indian
30.	Buenos Aires
31.	true
32.	false
33.	true
34.	false
35.	false
36.	false
37.	false
38.	false
39.	true
40.	false
41.	false
42.	true
43.	true
44.	true
45.	true
46.	true
47.	false
48.	false
49.	false
50.	false

ALTERNATE LIFEPAC TEST

1.	K
2.	A
3.	U
4.	A
5.	A
6.	K
7.	U
8.	K
9.	K
10.	A
11.	U
12.	A
13.	U
14.	K
15.	U
16.	A
17.	e
18.	i
19.	p
20.	n
21.	c
22.	l
23.	m
24.	f
25.	s
16.	d
27.	t
28.	o
29.	j
30.	r
31.	g
32.	a
33.	k
34.	h
35.	b
36.	q
37.	false
38.	false
39.	false
40.	true
41.	true
42.	true
43.	false
44.	true
45.	true
46.	true
47.	true
48.	false

HISTORY & GEOGRAPHY 404

ALTERNATE LIFEPAC TEST

NAME _____

DATE _____

SCORE _____

80
100

Put a *U* if the statement is about Ukraine, a *K* if it is about Kenya, and an *A* for Argentina (3 points each answer).

1. _____ on the equator

2. _____ most of the country is south of the Tropic of Capricorn

3. _____ most of the people are part of the Eastern Orthodox Church

4. _____ most of the people are part of the Roman Catholic Church

5. _____ was one of the wealthiest countries in the world in the early 1900s

6. _____ the grassland is mostly savanna

7. _____ country north of the Black Sea, southwest of Russia

8. _____ country famous for safaris, can see animals such as elephants, lions, and giraffes

9. _____ country where everyone wants to have a *shambas* on his tribe's land

10. _____ *los desaparecidos* disappeared under military rule

11. _____ called the "Breadbasket of Europe"

12. _____ country only 600 miles from Antarctica, southernmost town is there

13. _____ was a communist country until 1991

14. _____ had a one-party government under Jamo Kenyatta

15. _____ many of the small farmers became serfs when Poland ruled the country

16. _____ gauchos are a part of the national folklore

Match these items (2 points each answer).

17. _____ Patagonia

18. _____ Falkland

19. _____ Cossack

20. _____ Nairobi

21. _____ Chernobyl

22. _____ Crimea

23. _____ Kiev

24. _____ Dnepr

25. _____ Pampas

26. _____ Andes

27. _____ Victoria

28. _____ Buenos Aires

29. _____ Mombasa

30. _____ Ushuaia

31. _____ Mau Mau

32. _____ Swahili

33. _____ Britain

34. _____ USSR

35. _____ Spain

36. _____ Tierra del Fuego

a. Bantu and Arab culture/language

b. country that ruled Argentina

c. nuclear power plant disaster

d. mountains in Argentina

e. dry plateau of steppes in south Argentina

f. river in Ukraine

g. revolt in Kenya

h. country that ruled Ukraine

i. islands near Argentina, war fought with Britain over them

j. African east coast city/state

k. country that ruled Kenya

l. peninsula in southern Ukraine

m. capital of Ukraine

n. capital of Kenya

o. capital of Argentina

p. Ukrainian peasant soldier

q. island south of Argentina, "land of fire"

r. southernmost town in the world

s. rich grassland of Argentina

t. Kenyan lake, source of the Nile River

Write *true* or *false* on the blank (1 point each answer).

37. _____ There are about 6 different tribes in Kenya.

38. _____ Most of the people in Argentina are mestizo.

39. _____ Kenya's grasslands are the source of the country's wealth of crops.

40. _____ Many of the food crops people grow are grasses.

41. _____ Ukraine is rich in mineral resources.

42. _____ Savannas have a wet and dry season, but temperatures do not change much.

43. _____ Fire is very harmful to wild grasslands.

44. _____ Wheat is an important product of both Argentina and Ukraine.

45. _____ Cattle are raised on all of the three countries' grasslands.

46. _____ An icon is a religious picture of Jesus, Mary, or person of faith.

47. _____ Soccer is a popular sport in all three grassland countries.

48. _____ Kenya is a wealthy, developed country.

HISTORY & GEOGRAPHY 405

Unit 5: Tropical Rain Forests

TEACHER NOTES

MATERIALS NEEDED FOR LIFEPAC	
Required	Suggested
• dictionary • encyclopedia • atlas, maps, globe • crayons, colored pencils or markers (the reference materials can be either in book or online formats)	• map of South America • pictures of float plane • map of Africa • pictures of jungle animals and products

ADDITIONAL LEARNING ACTIVITIES

Section 1: Rain forests of the World
1. Have the students make a poster of animals found in rain forests.
2. Discuss the controversy of the rain forests being endangered.
3. Color where rain forests are located on a blank world map.

Section 2: The Amazon Rain Forest
1. Map drills. Show the Amazon River and the Congo River. Let the students see that the mouth of the Amazon is just across the Atlantic from the mouth of the Congo.
2. Arrange an assembly for the school and show a film or video on missionary aviation.
3. Take a field trip to a zoo to see animals of the tropics.
4. Draw and color a map of South America and label the equator and the Amazon River.

Section 3: The Congo Rain Forest
1. Have a missionary from Congo come and talk to the class.
2. Dramatize "Stanley Finds Livingstone" or "Livingstone's Death."
3. Carve a dugout from a small branch of wood.
4. Draw jungle plants and animals.
5. Draw and color an outline map of Africa. Label the equator and the Congo River.

ADDITIONAL INFORMATION

The name Congo is still used by a little republic west of the Congo River. After World War II the colonies in Africa started gaining independence. In 1960 part of French Equatorial Africa became the Congo Republic. A little later in 1960 the Belgian Congo became the independent Republic of the Congo. In 1971 this larger Republic of the Congo became Zaire. English and Belgian names were all changed to African names. In 1997 the country was renamed to the *Democratic Republic of the Congo*. Quarrels among tribal leaders and foreign agitators, seeking the mineral wealth of the southern hills, have kept Congo from making much progress.

Livingstone and Stanley were both explorers, but their purposes were so different. Livingstone names the places he discovered for his queen, Victoria. Stanley named places after himself. Livingstone loved the Africans. His purpose was to help them, to rescue them from the slave traders, and to tell them the "Good News." Stanley did not like the Africans and treated them with disdain. He explored because he was paid for his services. He admired the great Livingstone, but lacked Christian love for the natives.

The impact of Christian missions on Congo is lauded by secular writers. Before the missionaries went to Congo there were no words in the language for brotherhood, charity, forgiveness, duty, and justice. These concepts were alien to their way of life. Christianity demonstrated the meaning of these words and they became a part of the vocabulary in Congo.

The Amazon jungle was traversed three hundred years before the jungle of the Congo was explored. Yet, education in the Amazon is still behind the schooling of Congo. The Amazon did not have a David Livingstone to inspire a flood of missionaries.

The flag of the United States in 1871, which Stanley carried in his search for Livingstone, had thirty-seven stars.

ADDITIONAL ACTIVITY

This activity can be a creative expression, rather than verbal, of what the student has learned in this LIFEPAC to supplement your evaluation of his achievement. The activity could also be used before the final test to clarify similarities and differences in the two regions.

This activity could also be used with groups and used for display having the group explain its drawing to the rest of the class.

Administer the LIFEPAC Test.

The test is to be administered in one session. Give no help except with directions.
Evaluate the tests and review areas where the students have done poorly.
Review the pages and activities that stress the concepts tested.
If necessary, administer the Alternate LIFEPAC Test.

STUDENT INSTRUCTIONS

Draw and color two pictures. Label one the *Amazon River* and the other the *Congo River*. Show native people on or near each river, animals, plants, houses, and anything more that will help to tell what life is like along each river. Things that are nearly the same and those that are different should easily be seen.

ANSWER KEYS

SECTION 1

1.1-1.4 Teacher check
1.5 Any order: Latin America, Central Africa, Southeast Asia
1.6 Amazon River
1.7 equator
1.8 hot, regular (or heavy)
1.9 80
1.10 b
1.11 e
1.12 c
1.13 d
1.14 a
1.15 poor
1.16 temperate zone
1.17 many
1.18 species
1.19 light
1.20 From the plants and animals that die and fall to the forest floor.
1.21 The trees put the water back into the air through small holes in their leaves.
1.22 h
1.23 g
1.24 i
1.25 c
1.26 a
1.27 d
1.28 f
1.29 b
1.30 e
1.31 Any order:
hunter/gatherers, slash and burn farmers
1.32 poisoned
1.33 burning
1.34 forest again
1.35 An area the size of West Virginia
1.36 By roads built by governments or businesses
1.37 They sell or leave the fields and move on to clear more forest land.
1.38 Any order:
a. the climate may get warmer
b. less rain will fall in the forest region
1.39 Any six: coffee, chocolate, bananas, corn, tea, sweet potatoes, Brazil nuts, rubber, tapioca, mahogany, teak, balsa, drugs
1.40 Teacher check

SELF TEST 1

1.01 i
1.02 h
1.03 c
1.04 j
1.05 b
1.06 d
1.07 a
1.08 e
1.09 f
1.010 g
1.011-1.015 Give partial credit
1.011 Either order:
a. hot temperatures
b. regular rainfall
1.012 Any order:
a. Latin America
b. Central Africa
c. Southeast Asia
1.013 The plants and animals that die, fall to the ground, and are recycled into the soil.
1.014 Either order:
a. hunter/gatherers
b. slash and burn farmers
1.015 Burn the dead plants and trees after they cut them down
1.016 understory
1.017 drugs
1.018 equator
1.019 tropics
1.020 canopy
1.021 species
1.022 cattle ranches
1.023 floor
1.024 roads
1.025 Mahogany
1.026 false
1.027 true
1.028 true
1.029 false
1.030 false
1.031 true
1.032 true
1.033 false
1.034 false

SECTION 2

2.1	toward the east
2.2	no
2.3	Any three: Brazil, Peru, Colombia, Venezuela, Guyana, Suriname, French Guiana
2.4	Iquitos and Manaus
2.5	Black River
2.6	River Sea
2.7	Belem
2.8	d
2.9	b
2.10	e
2.11	g
2.12	c
2.13	a
2.14	f
2.15	It floods for miles in every direction.
2.16	The fish eat the tree's fruit and spread the seeds.
2.17	women fighters or warriors
2.18	a. Francisco de Orelana b. El Dorado
2.19	a. Brazilwood b. red
2.20	rubber
2.21	Any order: Portugal, Spain
2.22	1660
2.23	Vulcanizing
2.24	Any three: Brazil nuts, turtle oil, cocoa, fragrant oils, fish, wood, rubber
2.25	1870 to 1913
2.26	debt slavery
2.27	Manaus
2.28	tires
2.29	Asian rubber trees could be grown together on plantations. Amazon trees were spread out all over the forest.
2.30	true
2.31	false
2.32	true
2.33	false
2.34	false
2.35	false
2.36	false
2.37	FUNAI
2.38	cruel
2.39	diseases
2.40	culture
2.41	land
2.42	Marechal Candido Rondon started the SPI to contact the forest Indians and prepare them to meet the modern world.
2.43	They bring medicine, education, and teach the Indians about Jesus.
2.44	They farm small gardens and hunt or gather in the forest.

SELF TEST 2

2.01	f
2.02	i
2.03	b
2.04	e
2.05	d
2.06	h
2.07	j
2.08	a
2.09	c
2.010	g

2.011-2.015 Give partial credit

2.011 Any order:
 a. canopy
 b. understory
 c. floor

2.012 It floods.

2.013 They could raise their trees on plantations while the Brazilians could not.

2.014 The soil is very poor. It gets its nutrients from the dying plants and animals of the forest. When the forest is cut down the soil is not fertile

2.015 Any order:
 a. Latin America
 b. Central Africa
 c. Southeast Asia

2.016	FUNAI
2.017	debt slavery
2.018	sloth
2.019	hoatzin
2.020	ecotourism
2.021	latex
2.022	piranha
2.023	anaconda
2.024	Orchids
2.025	El Dorado
2.026	true
2.027	false
2.028	false
2.029	true
2.030	true
2.031	false
2.032	true
2.033	true
2.034	true

SECTION 3

3.1	equator

3.2 Any five:
Republic of the Congo, D.R. Congo, Central African Republic, Gabon, Cameroon, Equatorial Guinea

3.3	Lualaba

3.4 Any order:
 a. Matadi
 b. Kinshasa
 c. Kisangani

3.5	Malebo
3.6	Atlantic
3.7	false
3.8	true
3.9	false
3.10	false
3.11	a
3.12	d
3.13	b
3.14	a
3.15	c
3.16	c
3.17	d
3.18	b
3.19	c
3.20	d
3.21	true
3.22	true
3.23	false
3.24	false
3.25	true
3.26	true
3.27	true
3.28	false
3.29	false
3.30	Teacher check

3.31 The army rebelled and a civil war began.

3.32 The government has not made roads into the rain forest.

3.33 The government has not protected the animals.

3.34 Christian churches and missionaries

3.35 Mobutu

3.36 The people in the government stole everything.

3.37 They belong to many different tribes and cultures.

3.38	Catholic
3.39	mud; leaves
3.40	riverboats
3.41	Catholic Church
3.42	Bantu

3.43   farming small plots and hunting or fishing

3.44   basket traps

3.45   Any order: plantains, manioc

3.46   Any order: Efe, Mbuti

3.47   Any order: trees, vines, leaves

3.48   farmers

3.49   government

3.50   Any order: termites, honey

3.51   hunters

3.52   gardens

3.53   a. Nile

        b. Amazon

        c. about 4,200 miles

SELF TEST 3

3.01   AC

3.02   A

3.03   C

3.04   A

3.05   C

3.06   AC

3.07   A

3.08   C

3.09   A

3.010   AC

3.011   g

3.012   j

3.013   a

3.014   b

3.015   d

3.016   f

3.017   e

3.018   c

3.019   h

3.020   i

3.021   C

3.022   B

3.023   C

3.024   C

3.025   C

3.026   B

3.027   C

3.028   B

3.029   B

3.030   B

3.031-3.034 Give partial credit.

3.031   The army rebelled and a civil war started.

3.032   Christian churches and missionaries

3.033   Trade with merchants on the riverboats

3.034   From the forest and trade with farmers; food includes fruits, insects, meat, fish, nuts, berries, and honey

3.035   true

3.036   true

3.037   false

3.038   true

3.039   false

3.040   false

3.041   true

LIFEPAC TEST

I.	El Dorado		40.	true
2.	FUNAI		41.	false
3.	canopy		42.	true
4.	debt slavery		43.	true
5.	slash and burn		44.	true
6.	hunter/gatherers		45.	true
7.	understory			
8.	tropics			
9.	Missionaries			
10.	Ecotourism			

11.-15. (give partial credit)

11. Asian trees could be grown on plantations. In Brazil they had to be spread out through the forest.

12. Any order:
   a. Latin America
   b. Central Africa
   c. Southeast Asia

13. Mobutu and other government officials stole so much money that they ruined the country. There was no money to run businesses, schools, hospitals, or other things.

14. The soil is very poor. It gets its nutrients from the dying plants and animals of the forest. When the forest is cut down, the soil is not fertile.

15. They treated the people cruelly by enslaving and killing them.

16. C
17. C
18. A
19. AC
20. AC
21. A
22. A
23. A
24. C
25. C
26. h
27. j
28. b
29. e
30. d
31. g
32. c
33. i
34. f
35. a
36. false
37. false
38. false
39. true

ALTERNATE LIFEPAC TEST

l.	g	27.	false
2.	b	28.	true
3.	a	29.	true
4.	e	30.	false
5.	i	31.	C
6.	c	32.	AC
7.	f	33.	AC
8.	d	34.	A
9.	h	35.	A
10.	j	36.	AC
11.	Henry Stanley	37.	A
12.	Mobutu	38.	C
13.	Kinshasa	39.	C
14.	El Dorado	40.	C

15. Belgium
16. Andes
17. Rio Negro
18. Portugal
19. tropics
20. Amazon
21. true
22. false
23. false
24. true
25. false
26. true

(give partial credit on 41-44)

41. The soil is very poor. It gets its nutrients from the dying plants and animals of the forest. When the forest is cut down, the soil is not fertile.

42. More water flows out of it than any other river in the world.

43. They have kept some of the schools and hospitals open.

44. They gather and hunt in the forest. They also trade with or work for farming tribes for food.

HISTORY & GEOGRAPHY 405

ALTERNATE LIFEPAC TEST

NAME _____

DATE _____

SCORE _____

Match these items (2 points each answer).

1. _____ army ants
2. _____ manioc
3. _____ rubber
4. _____ piranha
5. _____ ivory
6. _____ sloth
7. _____ tapir
8. _____ tree frog
9. _____ hoatzin
10. _____ gorilla

a. product that made Manaus a rich city
b. food plant
c. lives and eats upside down
d. lay eggs in pools of water in air plants
e. tropical fish with very sharp teeth
f. pig-like; member of rhinoceros family
g. makes nests of their own bodies at night
h. tree-climbing bird
i. comes from elephant's tusks
j. largest of the apes

Using the words below, write the correct answers in the blanks (2 points each answer).

Portugal	Belgium	Andes	
Henry Stanley	Mobutu	Rio Negro	
Amazon	El Dorado	tropics	Kinshasa

11. _____ explored the Congo.

12. _____ became dictator of Congo and ruined the country.

13. _____ is a city in Congo.

14. The Spanish who explored the Amazon were searching for _____ .

15. Congo was a colony of _____ .

16. The source of the Amazon is in the _____ Mountains.

17. _____ is a tributary of the Amazon River.

18. Brazil was a colony of _____ .

19. The area between the Tropic of Cancer and the Tropic of Capricorn is called the
_____ .

20. The _____ was named after women warriors in Greek stories.

Write *true* or *false* on the blank (2 points each answer).

21. _____ Stanley was sent to Africa to find the missionary, David Livingstone.

22. _____ Very few species of plants and animals are in the rain forest.

23. _____ The highest level of the rain forest, the tree tops, are called the understory.

24. _____ Orchids are one kind of air plant that do not need soil.

25. _____ Amazon Indians seldom move to a new place.

26. _____ The people of the Congo are from many tribes that do not often trust each other.

27. _____ The anaconda is a small poisonous snake.

28. _____ The Amazon Indians raise crops in small clearings.

29. _____ Rubber collectors were forced to stay at their jobs by debt slavery.

30. _____ One major region of rain forest is in western Europe.

Write *A* on the line if the statement is about the Amazon region, *C* if it is about the Congo, and *AC* if it is true of both (3 points each answer).

31. _____ The river is navigable for long distances above the waterfalls that stop ocean ships.

32. _____ The river empties into the Atlantic Ocean.

33. _____ The region is wet and hot.

34. _____ The land near the river is flooded every wet season.

35. _____ Government roads are being used to destroy large areas of the rain forest.

36. _____ The people of the region were treated very badly by the Europeans.

37. _____ Piranhas and sloths live there.

38. _____ Pygmies and pygmy chimpanzees live there.

39. _____ The river crosses the equator twice.

40. _____ The region is located in Africa.

Answer these questions.

41. Why is rain forest land not good for crops or cattle ranching? (4 points) _____

_____

_____

42. Why is the Amazon called the largest river system in the world? (2 points) _____

_____

_____

43. How have Christian missionaries helped the people of the Congo? (2 points) _____

_____

_____

44. Where and how do the pygmies get their food? (2 points) _____

_____

_____

HISTORY & GEOGRAPHY 406

Unit 6: The Polar Regions

TEACHER NOTES

MATERIALS NEEDED FOR LIFEPAC	
Required	Suggested
• dictionary • encyclopedia • atlas, maps, globe • crayons, colored pencils or markers (the reference materials can be either in book or online formats)	(None)

ADDITIONAL LEARNING ACTIVITIES

Section 1: The Polar Regions

1. Map drills

   a. Show the class the Arctic Ocean and the land around it. Let pupils name the continents.

   b. Point out the continent of Antarctica with the water around it. Let the pupils name the oceans.

   c. Locate on a globe all the places mentioned in the story. The Ob River is one of the great rivers of the world. Make tag cards for the new places and add them to the geography fish pond.

2. Demonstrations

   a. Use a flashlight in a darkened room to show on the chalkboard the area covered by the light, when the rays are slanted. Compare this area with the area held directly toward the board (at a 90° angle). The same amount of light (and heat) is spread over a much larger area when the rays are slanted. Therefore, the slanting rays of the sun which reach the polar regions are less warming per unit of surface than the rays which strike the earth closer to the equator.

   b. Float a piece of ice in a glass container and observe the portion of the ice that is underwater. So it is with the iceberg—most of its mass is submerged.

3. Write a report on the *Titanic*.

Section 2: The Arctic Polar Region

1. Discuss these questions with your class.

   a. How has God provided protection for the Arctic animals? (protective coloration to match their surroundings)

   b. How do the fears of Lapp children compare with the fears of American city children? (Is a pack of wolves more dreaded than a gang of vandalizing hoodlums?)

2. Let groups in the class make dioramas portraying the reindeer-oriented life of the Lapps. (Matchsticks make "log" houses and churches. Christmas reindeer supply the animals.)

3. Write reports on these topics:
   Different Arctic Explorers
   The *Nautilus*

Section 3: The Antarctic Polar Region

1. Discussion on the balance of nature—What's the result of killing off the whales in the Antarctic region? (The krill, food of the whales, is in oversupply.)

2. Have a radio broadcast to review the big events of the polar regions. Divide the class into groups of two or three people. Assign each group a date on which something exciting happened. Here are some suggested dates:

Date	Hint
December 14, 1911	What did Amundsen do?
April 15, 1912	Remember the pointed iceberg?

Review the LIFEPAC to find the story of each event. Look up more information in the encyclopedia, other books, or online.

Prepare a short newscast for a class program. Example: April 6, 1909—Today, Robert Peary, an officer in the United States Navy, reached the North Pole. For twenty-three years he's been making trips toward the top of the world. He finally reached the pole with the help of some Eskimos and Matthew Henson, an African American companion, who is an expert in handling dog teams. I am happy to report this great success. It was the result of people from three races working together. This is your newscaster Mary Doe.

3. Game of Review. Have each student write one question and its answer about anything in this section (or LIFEPAC). Divide the group into two teams. Choose one student to ask questions. Rules for this review game are the same as for a spelling bee. (Teacher may want to add some questions for a more thorough review.) The team or person to answer the most questions correctly is the winner.

ADDITIONAL ACTIVITIES

The first activity is a review of facts and can be successfully completed several ways. The student should be able to substantiate the correctness of his answers.

The second activity is a spelling exercise which also gives an indication if the student has knowledge enough of each word to classify it. This activity will be fun for accelerated students. Slower students could work together.

Answer Key:

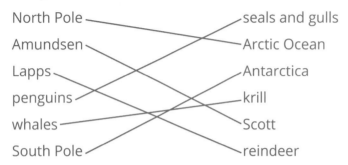

North Pole
Amundsen
Lapps
penguins
whales
South Pole

seals and gulls
Arctic Ocean
Antarctica
krill
Scott
reindeer

Explorers: Byrd, Amundsen, Scott, Hudson

Animals: penguin, krill, reindeer, walrus

Places: Prudhoe Bay, Antarctica, Lapland, Alaska

Administer the LIFEPAC Test.

> The test is to be administered in one session. Give no help except with directions.
> Evaluate the tests and review areas where the students have done poorly.
> Review the pages and activities that stress the concepts tested.
> If necessary, administer the Alternate LIFEPAC Test.

Draw a line to connect the words that go together.

North Pole	seals and gulls
Amundsen	Arctic Ocean
Lapps	Antarctica
penguins	krill
whales	Scott
South Pole	reindeer

Unscramble the words below and write each one in the correct box.

1. hoeduPr yBa
2. Bdry
3. guePnni
4. ttoSc
5. Aaaittnrcc
6. aksalA

7. rlliK
8. ndumnesA
9. Llaapdn
10. Rreeeind
11. Hsonud
12. Wsurla

```
Explorers
_____
_____
_____
_____
```

```
Animals
_____
_____
_____
_____
```

```
Places
_____
_____
_____
_____
```

ANSWER KEYS

SECTION 1

1.1	a.	North Pole
	b.	Arctic Circle
	c.	Antarctic Circle
	d.	South Pole
1.2	winter	
1.3	sun	
1.4	slanted	
1.5	Arctic (Antarctic) Circle	
1.6	Northern Lights	
1.7	South Magnetic Pole	
1.8	deserts	
1.9	I	
1.10	G	
1.11	P	
1.12	P	
1.13	G	
1.14	I	
1.15	P	
1.16	I	
1.17	G	
1.18	true	
1.19	false	
1.20	false	
1.21	false	

SELF TEST 1

1.01	c
1.02	e
1.03	d
1.04	a
1.05	b
1.06	Arctic Circle
1.07	land
1.08	Southern Lights
1.09	Magnetic
1.010	ice
1.011	c
1.012	b
1.013	b
1.014	c
1.015	a
1.016	a
1.017	c
1.018	a
1.019	b
1.020	c
1.021	true
1.022	true
1.023	false
1.024	true
1.025	false
1.026	The owners believed the ship could not be sunk.
1.027	The earth is tilted toward the sun in the north during the summer.
1.028	They are covered with ice at the poles, have six months of light and darkness, are as dry as a desert, have lights in the sky from the magnetic poles, are surrounded by pack ice that grows in the winter, and both produce icebergs. (Give partial credit).
1.029	A piece of a glacier falls off—it is called calving.

SECTION 2

2.1	b
2.2	a
2.3	d
2.4	c
2.5	Greece
2.6	Henry Hudson
2.7	Northwest Passage
2.8	1906
2.9	pack ice
2.10	Robert Peary, Matthew Henson, and four Eskimos (Inuit)
2.11	The *Nautilus* was the first ship to reach the North Pole. It was a submarine and sailed under the ice.
2.12	Another man claimed to have gone to the Pole, but he had no proof. Peary was able to use his notes to prove he had been there.
2.13	Richard Byrd and Floyd Bennett
2.14	That it was an island
2.15	By dogsled
2.16	Greenland
2.17	bigger
2.18	North America, Europe, Asia
2.19	permafrost
2.20	tundra
2.21	wet
2.22	treeline
2.23	continental glacier
2.24	false
2.25	true
2.26	true
2.27	false
2.28	false
2.29	a. Any one: fish, birds' eggs, seaweed, dead whales, seals, or walrus b. Any one: bears' leftovers, lemmings, voles, rabbits c. plants or rootsd. d. plants or roots e. lemmings or voles f. grass or lichens g. grass or lichens h. caribou or reindeer i. twigs or grass
2.30	Any order: a. snowy owl b. ptarmigan
2.31	Any three: geese, ducks, swans, loons, or terns
2.32	polar bear
2.33	lemmings

2.34	Teacher check
2.35	Teacher check
2.36	Any four: meat; food milk; drink or make cheese blood; soup or pancakes bones and antlers; knives, belt buckles sinews; thread stomachs; carry milk or cheese
2.37	Russia, Norway, Finland, Sweden
2.38	Sami
2.39	A sled pulled by reindeer.
2.40	Rifles, snowmobiles, helicopters, radios
2.41	Any order: a. harpoon b. kayak
2.42	igloo
2.43	eater of raw meat
2.44	Inuit
2.45	dogs
2.46	food
2.47	blubber lamp
2.48	He dug down to the permafrost, made a rock-lined pit, and covered it with more rocks.
2.49	He would find a seal's air hole, wait for the animal to return, and kill it.
2.50	They used skin boats, hit the whale with a harpoon attached to a sealskin float. When the whale got tired and came up again, they hit it again with harpoons and spears until it was dead.
2.51	false
2.52	true
2.53	true
2.54	false
2.55	false
2.56	false

SELF TEST 2

2.01 Arctic
2.02 Antarctic
2.03 North Magnetic Pole
2.04 treeline
2.05 tundra
2.06 e
2.07 b
2.08 a
2.09 c
2.010 d
2.011-2.012 (Give partial credit as needed).
2.011 They went out in skin boats. They hit the whale with a harpoon attached to sealskin floats. When the whale tired of pulling the floats, it surfaced and was hit again until they killed it.
2.012 Both poles are covered with ice; the pack ice grows each winter; they are as dry as a desert; they have lights in their skies from the magnetic poles; they produce icebergs.
2.013 pack ice
2.014 Lichens
2.015 Northwest Passage
2.016 *Nautilus*
2.017 permafrost
2.018 Siberia
2.019 Southern Lights
2.020 petroleum
2.021 glacier
2.022 icebergs
2.023 L
2.024 E
2.025 E & L
2.026 E
2.027 E & L
2.028 E & L
2.029 L
2.030 L
2.031 E
2.032 E
2.033 false
2.034 false
2.035 true
2.036 false
2.037 false
2.038 true
2.039 false
2.040 true
2.041 true
2.042 true

SECTION 3

3.1 a blank
3.2 Captain James Cook
3.3 seals
3.4 Any order:
   a. draw a picture of it
   b. put it on a map
   c. give it a name
3.5 true
3.6 false
3.7 false
3.8 true
3.9 Any order:
   a. South Pole
   b. South Magnetic Pole
3.10 a ship
3.11 long days of darkness
3.12 British
3.13 dogs
3.14 Ernest Shackleton
3.15 Robert Scott
3.16 Any order:
   a. Roald Amundsen, Norway
   b. Robert Scott, Great Britain
3.17 He died on the way back from leading the second expedition to reach the South Pole.
3.18 Richard Byrd
3.19 1958
3.20 They agreed not to do anything about their land claims, use the continent only for peaceful, scientific research, and to share what they learn.
3.21 Roald Amundsen
3.22-3.26 Teacher check
3.27 c
3.28 d
3.29 a
3.30 b
3.31 Cold air cannot hold much moisture.
3.32 It never melts. It packs down to form thick ice.
3.33 Downhill, to the ocean
3.34 Any order:
   a. It is higher in altitude.
   b. It is on land.
3.35 krill
3.36 no
3.37 baleen
3.38 Any order: moss, lichens
3.39 blubber
3.40 d
3.41 a
3.42 b

3.43   e
3.44   c
3.45   Any order:
    a. thick blubber
    b. overlapping feathers
    c. waterproof oil coating
    d. down, under the feathers
3.46   rookery
3.47   He puts it on his foot and covers it with his belly. He keeps it for two months like that without eating.
3.48   snowmobiles
3.49   scientists
3.50   moves
3.51   Any order: airplanes, icebreakers
3.52   vacation
3.53   freeze
3.54   Teacher check

SELF TEST 3

3.01   a
3.02   f
3.03   c
3.04   b
3.05   g
3.06   d
3.07   e
3.08   true
3.09   true
3.010 true
3.011 false
3.012 true
3.013 true
3.014 false
3.015 true
3.016 true
3.017 true
3.018 They have six months of light and darkness; poles covered with ice; Northern or Southern Lights; pack ice that grows and shrinks each year; produces icebergs.
3.019 People live in the Arctic, not in the Antarctic; there are no land animals in Antarctica; Antarctica is colder; Arctic has land around the edges and ocean at the poles, the Antarctic has land at the pole and oceans around the edges.
3.020 unknown southern land
3.021 seals
3.022 long days of darkness
3.023 dogsleds
3.024 north
3.025 Penguins
3.026 Lapps
3.027 Eskimos
3.028 continental glacier
3.029 krill
3.030 Northwest Passage
3.031 Amundsen-Scott
3.032 Antarctic Convergence
3.033 Musk oxen
3.034 Operation Highjump
3.035 pack ice
3.036 an iceberg
3.037 seals
3.038 Siberia

LIFEPAC TEST

1. N
2. S
3. N
4. S
5. S
6. N
7. S
8. S
9. N
10. S
11. j
12. a
13. d
14. e
15. h
16. g
17. i
18. c
19. b
20. f
21. Northern Lights
22. Eskimos (Inuit)
23. Antarctic Circle
24. winter
25. Lapps (Sami)
26. Henry Hudson
27. long days of darkness
28. continental glacier
29. pack ice
30. South Magnetic Pole
31. seals
32. *Nautilus*
33. dogs
34. icebergs
35. deserts
36. packed snow
37. Roald Amundsen
38. Richard Byrd
39. move downhill
40. south

ALTERNATE LIFEPAC TEST

1. e
2. a
3. b
4. d
5. f
6. c
7. true
8. true
9. false
10. true
11. false
12. false
13. Antarctica
14. petroleum
15. Eskimo
16. Lapp (Sami)
17. tundra
18. krill
19. continental glacier
20. mosquitoes
21. Greenland
22. Amundsen-Scott
23. Siberia
24. b
25. c
26. d
27. a
28. B
29. N
30. N
31. B
32. S
33. B
34. S
35. B
36. N
37. S

HISTORY & GEOGRAPHY 406

ALTERNATE LIFEPAC TEST

NAME _____

DATE _____

SCORE _____

Match these items (2 points each answer).

1. _____ snowy owl
2. _____ musk ox
3. _____ penguin
4. _____ lemming
5. _____ caribou
6. _____ polar bear

a. the largest animal of the Arctic

b. a bird that swims instead of flies

c. the meat-eating king of the Arctic

d. a mouse-like animal

e. a bird whose winter color matches the snow

f. grass-eating Arctic deer

Write *true* or *false on the blank* (2 points each answer).

7. _____ The hardest part of an Antarctic winter is the long days of darkness.

8. _____ A crevasse is a deep, dangerous crack in a glacier.

9. _____ The Northwest Passage is a strait by the Antarctic Peninsula.

10. _____ The Antarctic Convergence is the end of the Antarctic region.

11. _____ The first ship to the North Pole was a huge ice breaker.

12. _____ The ice on a glacier comes from frozen sea water.

From the list of words below choose words to complete the sentences (4 points each answer).

Amundsen-Scott	Greenland	Siberia
Lapps (Sami)	Eskimo	Antarctica
petroleum	krill	mosquitoes
continental glacier	tundra	

13. The last place on earth to be explored and mapped was _____ .

14. The most important mineral of the Arctic is _____ .

15. The _____ name means "eaters of raw meat."

16. The nomads who live off their reindeer herd are _____ .

17. The treeless Arctic plain is called the _____ .

18. Tiny shrimp-like animals of the Antarctic region are called _____ .

19. Antarctica has a storehouse of fresh water in its _____ .

20. In summer the Arctic region is pestered with _____ .

21. A large glacier covers the island of _____ .

22. The _____ Base used to be right on the South Pole.

23. The Arctic part of Russia is called _____ .

Match these items (3 points each answer).

24. _____ Henry Hudson

25. _____ Roald Amundsen

26. _____ Richard Byrd

27. _____ Robert Scott

a. He died on his return from being the second person at the South pole.

b. He was looking for a passage around America in the 1600s.

c. He was first to reach the South Pole.

d. He was the first man to fly over the North and South Poles.

Write _N_ in the blank if the statement or thing is from the North Polar region, _S_ if it is from the South Polar region, and _B_ if it is both (2 points each answer).

28. _____ Dry as a desert

29. _____ Many large land animals

30. _____ Eskimos (Inuit) and Lapps (Sami) live there

31. _____ Has days in the summer when the sun never sets

32. _____ Penguins

33. _____ Surrounded by pack ice

34. _____ High altitude makes it the coldest place on earth

35. _____ Icebergs calve off the glaciers

36. _____ Pole is over the ocean

37. _____ First people to stay all winter lived on ships which were frozen in the ice

HISTORY & GEOGRAPHY 407

Unit 7: Mountain Countries

TEACHER NOTES

MATERIALS NEEDED FOR LIFEPAC	
Required	Suggested
• dictionary • encyclopedia • atlas, maps, globe • crayons, colored pencils or markers (the reference materials can be either in book or online formats)	• pictures of Peru (travel agencies or magazines) • postage stamps from Peru • products of Peru, such as potatoes, lima beans, cotton, sugar cane, copper, and alpaca sweaters • pictures of Switzerland • Swiss products such as clocks, watches, dotted swiss fabric, cheeses, fondue, lebkuchen, swiss skis, ski clothes, chocolate, the Red Cross, and music boxes

ADDITIONAL LEARNING ACTIVITIES

Section 1: Peru - The Andes

1. Discuss the great building achievements of the Inca Indians (pictures of some of the ruins would be helpful. They are available from travel agencies and magazines such as *National Geographic*).

2. Discuss the fishing industry. Compare Peru and Japan. Peru is the greater fishing nation due to the massive anchovy catches.

3. Invite a missionary or tourist to Peru to come and speak to the class.

4. Have the class collect pictures, artifacts, and products of Peru for a display.

5. Small groups could write and illustrate reports on the uses of llamas (beasts of burden, food, wool, and leather) and the process of making a wool poncho from llama fleece to a finished colorful product.

6. Write a paragraph about:
   a. the fishing industry of Peru,
   b. building railroads in the Andes,
   c. the Inca Indians, or
   d. hats, ponchos, and fiestas of Peru.

Section 2: Nepal - The Himalayas

1. Have the students draw a picture of Mt. Everest.

2. Discuss the differences in climate between the top of the Himalayan Mountains and the bottom.

3. Have the students report on the religions of Hinduism and Buddhism.

4. Pair up students and have them give a report on various expeditions to the top of Mt. Everest.

Section 3: Switzerland - The Alps

1. Discuss and compare the state-imposed Roman Catholic religion of Peru as it compares to the Protestant evangelical influence in Switzerland. (John Calvin; Ulrich Zwingli; Geneva Bible; meetings on world evangelism in Lausanne; Francis Schaeffer, noted theologian and Christian philosopher, founded a Christian community, L'Abri, in the Swiss Alps)

2. Discuss differences and similarities in religion and possible influences religion has had on each country's prosperity and progress.

3. Demonstrate to the class the making of cottage cheese.

4. Cheese tasting party. Different Swiss cheeses could be brought and sampled by the class to determine difference in taste. A report on cheese making could also be presented.

5. Bulletin board display on "The Playground of the World" could include ski resorts, clothes, equipment, towns, games, and so forth. Report on when the Winter Olympics were held in Switzerland or on the history of skiing.

6. Discuss the legend of William Tell (oral report) and play a recording of the "William Tell Overture" by Rossini.

7. Look up and compare on a graph the difference between the highest peaks of the Andes and the Alps.

8. Write a paragraph about
   a. a visit to Switzerland (in the form of a letter to your class),
   b. John Calvin, or
   c. the Geneva Bible.

9. Someone who is more interested in "doing" something rather than in "writing" could make these Swiss cookies, Lebkuchen, which are often holiday favorites in many American homes.

LEBKUCHEN[1]

1/2 cup honey	1/2 tsp. soda
1/2 cup molasses	1 tsp. cinnamon
3/4 cup brown sugar (packed)	1 tsp. cloves
1 egg	1 tsp. allspice
1 tbsp. lemon juice	1 tsp. nutmeg
1 tsp. grated lemon rind	1/3 cup cut-up citron
2 3/4 cups flour	1/3 cup chopped nuts
	Glazing Icing (recipe follows

Mix honey and molasses; bring to a boil. Stir in sugar, egg, lemon juice, and rind. Measure flour by dipping method. Stir dry ingredients together. Mix in citron and nuts. Chill dough overnight.

Heat oven to 400°. Roll small amount of dough at a time, keeping rest chilled. Roll out 1/4" thick on lightly floured board; cut in oblongs, 2-1/2" x 1-1/2". Place 1" apart on greased baking sheet. Bake 10 to 12 minutes or until no imprint remains when touched lightly. Brush icing lightly over cookies immediately. Quickly remove from baking sheet. Cool and store in airtight container with cut orange or apple for a few days to mellow. Makes 6 dozen cookies.

Glazing Icing

Blend 1 cup sugar and 1/2 cup water in small saucepan. Boil until first indication of thread appears (230° on candy thermometer). Remove from heat. Stir in 1/4 cup confectioners' sugar. If icing becomes sugary while brushing cookies, reheat slightly, adding a little water until clear again. Any leftover icing may be used on fruitcake or other fruit bars.

[1] Adapted from *Betty Crocker's Cook Book*, Golden Press, New York, 1963, by permission.

ADDITIONAL ACTIVITY

A puzzle has been added as either a supplementary activity, or for those students who might enjoy doing it for fun.

Answer Key for Puzzle

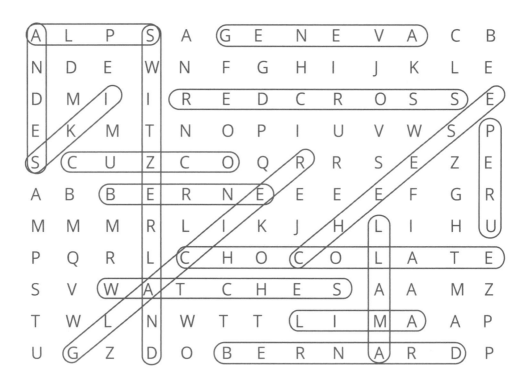

Administer the LIFEPAC Test.

> The test is to be administered in one session. Give no help except with directions.
> Evaluate the tests and review areas where the students have done poorly.
> Review the pages and activities that stress the concepts tested.
> If necessary, administer the Alternate LIFEPAC Test.

Find sixteen words in this puzzle about Peru and Switzerland. The following clues will help you.

```
A   L   P   S   A   G   E   N   E   V   A   C   B
N   D   E   W   N   F   G   H   I   J   K   L   E
D   M   I   I   R   E   D   C   R   O   S   S   E
E   K   M   T   N   O   P   I   U   V   W   S   P
S   C   U   Z   C   O   Q   R   R   S   E   Z   E
A   B   B   E   R   N   E   E   E   E   F   G   R
M   M   M   R   L   I   K   J   H   L   I   H   U
P   Q   R   L   C   H   O   C   O   L   A   T   E
S   V   W   A   T   C   H   E   S   A   A   M   Z
T   W   L   N   W   T   T   L   I   M   A   A   P
U   G   Z   D   O   B   E   R   N   A   R   D   P
```

1. St. _____ Pass in the Alps
2. July 28 is the Independence Day of _____ .
3. Camel of the mountains
4. The Inca Indians capital
5. The banks of _____ are very safe.
6. A large mass of ice
7. City with famous clock tower
8. Switzerland mountains
9. Swiss _____ ; best timepieces
10. Began in Geneva
11. Favorite sport of the Alps
12. Capital of Peru
13. Mountains of Peru
14. Palace of Nations is here
15. Two famous Swiss foods: _____ and _____

ANSWER KEYS

SECTION 1

1.1-1.3 Teacher check
1.4 Rockies, Appalachian
1.5 Andes
1.6 Alps, Pyrenees, Ural
1.7 Ethiopian Highlands, Atlas
1.8 Himalayas, Ural
1.9 Great Dividing Range
1.10 sea level
1.11 a. leafy trees
b. pine trees
c. tundra
d. snow and ice
1.12 Any order:
a. less air
b. cold
c. wind
d. less protection from the sun
1.13 tree line
1.14 snow line
1.15 change
1.16 adapt
1.17 Teacher check
1.18 desert
1.19 mountainous
1.20 rain forest
1.21 west or Pacific
1.22 Amazon
1.23 Lake Titicaca
1.24 minerals
1.25 Aconcagua
1.26 b
1.27 c
1.28 e
1.29 a

1.30 d
1.31 One third to the farmer, one third to the priests, and one third to the Incas.
1.32 Messengers waited at houses along the road. Each one ran the message quickly to the next house where another runner took it.
1.33 The people had to work for the king so many days each year.
1.34 They cut the blocks and fitted them together without mortar.
1.35 llamas
1.36 Any order: llamas, alpacas, vicuñas
1.37 vicuña
1.38 Any order: gold, silver
1.39 Francisco Pizzaro
1.40 false
1.41 false
1.42 true
1.43 false
1.44 false
1.45 false
1.46 true
1.47 true
1.48 true
1.49 true
1.50

Across	Down
3. Titicaca	1. quipu
6. Lima	2. airplane
7. copper	4. Amazon
9. sun	5. horse
10. Andes	6. Llama
	7. Cuzco
	8. Peru

SELF TEST 1

1.01 e
1.02 f
1.03 b
1.04 j
1.05 h
1.06 c
1.07 g
1.08 a
1.09 d
1.010 i
1.011 sun god
1.012 Francisco Pizzaro
1.013 Titicaca
1.014 llama
1.015 Cuzco
1.016 gold
1.017 quipu
1.018 vicuña
1.019 terraces
1.020 chuño
1.021 Any order:
    a. thin air
    b. cold
    c. wind
    d. less protection from sun
1.022 a. The climate changes as you go up a mountain.
    b. leafy trees
    c. snow and ice
1.023 In South America along the west coast
1.024 To build roads, buildings, and terraces
1.025 false
1.026 true
1.027 true
1.028 false
1.029 true
1.030 true
1.031 true
1.032 false
1.033 true
1.034 true

SECTION 2

2.1 Any order: Nepal, Bhutan
2.2 Any order: India, China
2.3 yak
2.4 Tibetan
2.5 sub-continent
2.6 the south
2.7 Mount Everest
2.8 rain forests
2.9 desert
2.10 China (Tibet)
2.11 India
2.12 Insects carried the disease malaria which kept people away until insecticides were invented.
2.13 Any order:
    a. Tarai—rain forest plains
    b. hills—heartland
    c. Himalayas—high mountains
2.14 eight
2.15 Any order:
    a. farming
    b. herding or raising animals
    c. trading
    d. being a mountain guide
2.16 b
2.17 a
2.18 d
2.19 c
2.20 true
2.21 false
2.22 true
2.23 false
2.24 true
2.25 Any order:
    a. people are reborn on earth after death
    b. many gods
    c. caste
2.26 Statues of gods or graven images
2.27 They will become part of the universe and disappear.
2.28 To get the god to do something for them or to do good deeds for a better next life.
2.29 Buddha
2.30 rebirth
2.31 gods
2.32 Jesus
2.33 wanting things
2.34 Sherpa
2.35 Any order: rice, maize, oilseed, jute, and sugar
2.36 Gurkha
2.37 farming

2.38 buckwheat, barley, and potatoes
2.39 Edmund Hillary and Tenzing Norgay
2.40 false
2.41 true
2.42 true
2.43 false
2.44 true
2.45 false
2.46 false

SELF TEST 2

2.01 a
2.02 h
2.03 j
2.04 b
2.05 d
2.06 i
2.07 e
2.08 c
2.09 f
2.010 g
2.011 N
2.012 P
2.013 N
2.014 N
2.015 N
2.016 P
2.017 N
2.018 P
2.019 P
2.020 P
2.021 The Spanish wanted the Inca gold and silver.
2.022 The most important animal is the yak which is used for food, wool, leather, and to carry things.
2.023 The llama is the most important animal because it is used for food, wool, and to carry things.
2.024 Any order:
a. Tarai (rain forest plains)
b. hills (heartland)
c. Himalayas (mountains)
2.025 false
2.026 false
2.027 true
2.028 false
2.029 true
2.030 true
2.031 false
2.032 false
2.033 true
2.034 true
2.035 Francisco Pizzaro
2.036 Rana
2.037 quipu
2.038 caste
2.039 Lima
2.040 Kathmandu
2.041 Cuzco
2.042 idols
2.043 Edmund Hillary or Tenzig Norgay
2.044 monsoon

SECTION 3

3.1	Bern
3.2	avalanche
3.3	Jura
3.4	Swiss Plateau
3.5	Blanc
3.6	Any order: Constance, Geneva
3.7	rivers
3.8	St. Bernard
3.9	Reformation
3.10	Helvetia
3.11	William Tell
3.12	Protestants
3.13	John Calvin; Zwingli
3.14	Thirty Years'
3.15	neutral
3.16	freedom
3.17	cantons
3.18	Austria
3.19	false
3.20	false
3.21	true
3.22	true
3.23	true
3.24	false
3.25	false
3.26	Teacher check
3.27	e
3.28	a
3.29	c
3.30	d
3.31	b
3.32	false
3.33	true
3.34	true
3.35	false
3.36	true
3.37	false
3.38	false

3.39 These items should be checked:

chocolate	cheese
banking	watches
tourism	electronic equipment

3.40
a. false
b. false
c. true
d. true
e. true

SELF TEST 3

3.01	e
3.02	i
3.03	d
3.04	a
3.05	b
3.06	j
3.07	f
3.08	c
3.09	g
3.010	h
3.011	Bern (or Berne)
3.012	Reformation
3.013	St. Bernard
3.014	cantons
3.015	rivers
3.016	neutral
3.017	Swiss Plateau
3.018	Constance
3.019	avalanche
3.020	Zwingli
3.021	Any three: German (Swiss German), French, Italian, Romansh
3.022	Switzerland
3.023	Nepal
3.024	Peru
3.025	Nepal
3.026	Peru
3.027	Switzerland
3.028	These should be checked: b, c, e, f, g
3.029	true
3.030	true
3.031	false
3.032	false
3.033	true
3.034	true
3.035	true
3.036	true
3.037	false
3.038	false
3.039	false
3.040	true
3.041	false

LIFEPAC TEST

1. S
2. P
3. N
4. P
5. S
6. N
7. N
8. S
9. S
10. S
11. P
12. S
13. N
14. N
15. P
16. b
17. c
18. d
19. e
20. f
21. h
22. j
23. a
24. g
25. i
26. Titicaca
27. Constance
28. Sherpa
29. Gurkha
30. William Tell
31. John Calvin
32. Lima
33. Francisco Pizzaro
34. (Sir) Edmund Hillary or Tenzing Norgay
35. St. Bernard
36. true
37. true
38. false
39. true
40. false
41. false
42. false
43. true
44. true
45. true
46. false
47. true

ALTERNATE LIFEPAC TEST

1. P
2. S
3. N
4. P
5. N
6. P
7. P
8. P
9. P
10. N
11. N
12. S
13. N
14. N
15. N
16. f
17. g
18. b
19. c
20. d
21. e
22. a
23. j
24. h
25. i
26. true
27. true
28. false
29. false
30. true
31. tundra
32. gold
33. vicuña
34. cheese
35. quipu
36. landlocked
37. Tourism
38. sea level
39. idols
40. monsoon

HISTORY & GEOGRAPHY 407

ALTERNATE LIFEPAC TEST

NAME _____

DATE _____

SCORE _____

80
100

Write _P_ in the blank if the sentence tells about Peru, write _S_ if it tells about Switzerland, and _N_ if it is about Nepal (3 points each answer).

1. _____ Spanish and Quechua are the languages.

2. _____ German, French, and Romansh are spoken.

3. _____ India is to the south and Tibet to the north.

4. _____ The Pacific Ocean is to the west and Brazil to the east.

5. _____ Each of about a hundred groups have their own language.

6. _____ Farmers still use terraces built by the Inca Empire.

7. _____ The capital is Lima.

8. _____ Lake Titicaca is here.

9. _____ Potatoes are an important crop and fishing an important industry.

10. _____ Mount Everest is here.

11. _____ Hinduism and Buddhism are important.

12. _____ Fine watches are made here.

13. _____ The Shah dynasty still rules here.

14. _____ The Sherpa people are well known as mountain guides.

15. _____ People here get milk and wool from yaks.

Match these items (2 points each answer).

16.	_____ a crossing through the Alps	a.	Himalayas
17.	_____ Empire that built Cuzco	b.	Andes
18.	_____ the mountains of Peru	c.	Geneva
19.	_____ the city of which John Calvin was the leader	d.	Bern
20.	_____ capital of Switzerland	e.	Kathmandu
21.	_____ capital of Nepal	f.	St. Bernard Pass
22.	_____ the mountains of Nepal	g.	Inca
23.	_____ the mountains of Switzerland	h.	Urals
24.	_____ mountains between Europe and Asia	i.	Amazon
25.	_____ river that starts in Peru	j.	Alps

Write *true* or *false on the blank* (1 point each answer).

26. _____ Climate changes as you climb up a mountain.

27. _____ The Inca was believed to be a god by his people.

28. _____ The Swiss Plateau is on the southern border of the country.

29. _____ The Jura Mountains are in Africa.

30. _____ Roman Catholicism is the most important religion of Peru.

Complete each sentence with a word from the list (3 points each answer).

tundra   monsoon   gold
vicuña   landlocked   tourism
cheese   quipu   idols
sea level

31. On a mountain _____ is between the tree line and the snow line.

32. The Incas thought _____ was the sweat of the sun.

33. Only the Inca royal family could wear clothes made from the wool of the _____ .

34. The Swiss are famous for their _____ which is made in modern factories.

35. The Incas used knotted strings called _____ to keep records.

36. Both Nepal and Switzerland are _____ countries.

37. _____ is an important source of income in Nepal and Switzerland.

38. Altitude is measured by the distance above _____ .

39. The people of Nepal worship _____ .

40. During the _____ , Nepal gets rain from the Indian Ocean.

HISTORY & GEOGRAPHY 408

Unit 8: Island Countries

TEACHER NOTES

MATERIALS NEEDED FOR LIFEPAC	
Required	Suggested
• dictionary • encyclopedia • atlas, maps, globe • crayons, colored pencils or markers (the reference materials can be either in book or online formats)	• book on origami, art of paper folding (library) • materials for volcano • music book with the tunes "Aloha Oe" and "Farewell to Thee"

ADDITIONAL LEARNING ACTIVITIES

Section 1: Cuba

1. Have the students bring products to class that are made from the crops grown in Cuba.

2. Have the students locate and label minerals that are found in Cuba.

3. Have the students draw a map of the islands of Cuba showing where they are in relation to the United States, Mexico and South America.

4. Make a chart showing the average rainfall for each month of the year in Cuba.

5. Write a report on the communistic government in Cuba.

Section 2: Iceland

1. Appoint a committee to build and demonstrate an erupting volcano.

2. Create a weather map for Iceland.

3. Make a poster of the animals that live in Iceland.

4. Write a report on one of the "sagas" of Iceland's past.

Section 3: Japan, A Country of Islands

1. Prepare a Japanese meal. Use your imagination. Form committees to plan and prepare the menu, the decorations, the placemats, the tables, pillows, chopsticks, and centerpieces. The menu should include rice, tea, vegetables, soy sauce, pickles, dried seaweed, and perhaps some shrimp. Eat at low tables while seated on pillows on the floor. Chopsticks could be used. Placemats could be made ahead of time by students, each one showing an aspect of Japanese life or a map of the islands. A Japanese flower arrangement for each table could be made by some students.

2. Japanese maps and flags. Drawings of the Japanese flag and important tourist places could be hung around the room.

3. Origami art. Decorations of origami art could hang from the ceiling.

4. Homemade Kite Flying Contest. Each student could make a kite at home out of materials gathered around the house. On a given day the kites could be brought to school and graded for originality and neatness. Then for fun a contest to determine which one will fly the best could be conducted and prizes given to the winners.

5. Make posters showing products "Made in Japan."

6. Extended Writing Assignment. Ideas for reports: Children's Festival
   Foods of Japan
   Products of Japan
   Kimonos and Pagodas

Administer the LIFEPAC Test.

The test is to be administered in one session. Give no help except with directions.
Evaluate the tests and review areas where the students have done poorly.
Review the pages and activities that stress the concepts tested.
If necessary, administer the Alternate LIFEPAC Test.

ANSWER KEYS

SECTION 1

1.1	e
1.2	d
1.3	a
1.4	b
1.5	c
1.6	e
1.7	b
1.8	d
1.9	a
1.10	c
1.11	a. east
	b. north
	c. west
	d. south
1.12	a. North America
	b. Australia
	c. Africa
	d. Asia
	e. South America
	f. Europe
	g. South America
	h. Africa
	i. Africa
1.13	c
1.14	d
1.15	a
1.16	b
1.17	false
1.18	false
1.19	true
1.20	Most of the Greater Antilles Islands are larger.
1.21-1.23	Teacher check
1.24	West Indies
1.25	Straits of Florida
1.26	Yucatán Channel
1.27	Windward Passage
1.28	Caribbean Sea
1.29	Antilles
1.30	Isle of Youth
1.31	sugar
1.32	tobacco; cigars
1.33	minerals
1.34	Havana
1.35	harbors
1.36	semi-tropical

1.37	moderate
1.38	dry
1.39	hurricane
1.40	true
1.41	false
1.42	false
1.43	false
1.44	true
1.45	false
1.46	true
1.47	
1.48	✓
1.49	✓
1.50	
1.51	
1.52	
1.53	United States
1.54	They tried to put missiles in Cuba to threaten the United States.
1.55	It was almost completely destroyed.
1.56	A lot of money.
1.57	They built boats and tried to escape.
1.58	e
1.59	c
1.60	b
1.61	a
1.62	d
1.63	f
1.64	The people do not get any reward for good work and the factory will not close for doing bad work.
1.65	No. People who are important in the government get better food, houses, and places to shop.
1.66	It is not easy to be a Christian in Cuba because of government persecution.
1.67	Any three: lively music, baseball, basketball, track and field
1.68	a. Africa
	b. Africa
	c. Central America
1.69	Fidel Castro
1.70	communist
1.71	soldiers
1.72	love
1.73	communists

SELF TEST 1

1.01	communist
1.02	tropical
1.03	coral reef
1.04	censorship
1.05	volcano
1.06	archipelago
1.07	islet
1.08	sea
1.09	barrier
1.010	lagoon
1.011	true
1.012	false
1.013	true
1.014	false
1.015	false
1.016	true
1.017	false
1.018	true
1.019	true
1.020	false
1.021	c
1.022	e
1.023	j
1.024	i
1.025	h
1.026	b
1.027	d
1.028	a
1.029	f
1.030	g
1.031	Fidel Castro
1.032	North America
1.033	hurricane
1.034	Columbus
1.035	Spain
1.036	United States
1.037	Europe
1.038	Cuba
1.039	Sugar
1.040	Tobacco

SECTION 2

2.1	d
2.2	c
2.3	j
2.4	b
2.5	g
2.6	a
2.7	f
2.8	e
2.9	h
2.10	i
2.11	geothermal; used to heat homes, buildings, and swimming pools
2.12	b
2.13	c
2.14	a
2.15	d
2.16	a
2.17	true
2.18	true
2.19	false
2.20	false
2.21	sagas
2.22	Irish monks
2.23	Vikings
2.24	Althing; A.D. 930
2.25	Norway and Denmark
2.26	They charged high prices for things from Europe and paid low prices for Icelandic goods.
2.27	to read and write
2.28	false
2.29	true
2.30	false
2.31	false
2.32	false
2.33	false
2.34	true
2.35	fishing
2.36	sheep
2.37	Any order: geothermal, hydroelectric
2.38	Norse
2.39	sagas
2.40	Your last name would be your father's first name plus "-sson" if you are a boy or "-sdottir" if you are a girl.
2.41	books
2.42	Evangelical Lutheran Church
2.43	fish and mutton
2.44	skyr
2.45	a woman

2.46 Any three:
ride horses, chess, card games, soccer, tests
of strength
2.47 expensive

SELF TEST 2

2.01 l
2.02 C
2.03 l
2.04 C
2.05 B
2.06 C
2.07 l
2.08 l
2.09 l
2.010 C
2.011 h
2.012 e
2.013 c
2.014 f
2.015 j
2.016 g
2.017 a
2.018 d
2.019 b
2.020 i
2.021 Gulf Stream
2.022 Great Britain
2.023 sagas
2.024 geothermal
2.025 Denmark
2.026 Althing
2.027 Arctic Circle
2.028 Skyr
2.029 hydroelectric
2.030 geyser
2.031 false
2.032 false
2.033 true
2.034 false
2.035 true
2.036 true
2.037 false
2.038 false
2.039 false
2.040 true
2.041 Barrier
2.042 islet
2.043 sheep
2.044 Atlantic
2.045 Columbus
2.046 Fidel Castro
2.047 books
2.048 atoll
2.049 volcanoes
2.050 Cuba

SECTION 3

3.1	Any order:	**3.41**	Diet
	Hokkaido, Honshu, Shikoku, Kyushu	**3.42**	Any order: U.S., China
3.2	Any order:	**3.43**	Akihito
	Sea of Japan, East China Sea, Sea of Okhotsk,	**3.44**	true
	Pacific Ocean	**3.45**	false
3.3	d	**3.46**	false
3.4	b	**3.47**	true
3.5	c	**3.48**	false
3.6	a	**3.49**	true
3.7	Fuji	**3.50**	true
3.8	Honshu	**3.51**	true
3.9	Montana	**3.52**	false
3.10	Tokyo	**3.53**	true
3.11	Inland Sea	**3.54**	false
3.12	false	**3.55**	✓
3.13	true	**3.56**	
3.14	true	**3.57**	✓
3.15	false	**3.58**	
3.16	true	**3.59**	
3.17	false	**3.60**	
3.18	false	**3.61**	✓
3.19	true	**3.62**	✓
3.20	e	**3.63**	✓
3.21	g	**3.64**	g
3.22	a	**3.65**	j
3.23	b	**3.66**	f
3.24	c	**3.67**	h
3.25	f	**3.68**	i
3.26	d	**3.69**	d
3.27	China	**3.70**	e
3.28	sun	**3.71**	b
3.29	Francis Xavier	**3.72**	c
3.30	Russo-Japanese	**3.73**	a
3.31	Europeans	**3.74**	true
3.32	trade or contact	**3.75**	true
3.33	conquer	**3.76**	true
3.34	Matthew Perry	**3.77**	false
3.35	Hirohito	**3.78**	false
3.36	Any order: Germany, Italy	**3.79**	Teacher check
3.37	Pearl Harbor	**3.80**	Teacher check
3.38	Midway		
3.39	atomic bombs		
3.40	Douglas MacArthur		

SELF TEST 3

3.01	J		**3.053**	true
3.02	I		**3.054**	true
3.03	J		**3.055**	true
3.04	C		**3.056**	false
3.05	C		**3.057**	true
3.06	I		**3.058**	false
3.07	J		**3.059**	false
3.08	J		**3.060**	false
3.09	I			
3.010	J			
3.011	J			
3.012	C			
3.013	J			
3.014	J			
3.015	I			
3.016	J			
3.017	C			
3.018	I			
3.019	C			
3.020	I			
3.021	j			
3.022	h			
3.023	a			
3.024	d			
3.025	i			
3.026	b			
3.027	c			
3.028	e			
3.029	g			
3.030	f			
3.031	Greenland			
3.032	Meiji			
3.033	Origami			
3.034	haiku			
3.035	Skyr			
3.036	Caribbean			
3.037	atoll			
3.038	Korea			
3.039	Bonsai			
3.040	tobacco			
3.041	false			
3.042	true			
3.043	true			
3.044	false			
3.045	true			
3.046	false			
3.047	true			
3.048	true			
3.049	true			
3.050	false			
3.051	true			
3.052	false			

LIFEPAC TEST

1. I
2. J
3. C
4. I
5. I
6. I
7. I
8. J
9. C
10. C
11. I
12. I
13. C
14. C
15. C
16. C
17. J
18. J
19. I
20. C
21. false
22. false
23. true
24. false
25. false
26. true
27. true
28. true
29. false
30. false
31. Teacher check:
The student should use facts from the LIFEPAC to explain his choice.
32. g
33. f
34. i
35. a
36. j
37. h
38. b
39. e
40. d
41. c
42. Fuji
43. Gulf Stream
44. Antilles
45. Surtsey
46. Youth
47. Madagascar
48. Nippon
49. Honshu
50. Tokyo
51. Indonesia

ALTERNATE LIFEPAC TEST

1. I
2. J
3. C
4. I
5. I
6. J
7. J
8. I
9. J
10. C
11. I
12. J
13. C
14. C
15. I
16. C
17. I
18. C
19. J
20. I
21. C
22. J
23. C
24. I
25. J
26. true

27. false
28. false
29. false
30. false
31. false
32. true
33. true
34. false
35. false
36. true
37. false
38. false
39. false
40. Havana
41. Meiji
42. Florida
43. Reykhavík
44. Greenland
45. Denmark
46. Madagascar
47. Fidel Castro
48. Nippon
49. Antilles
50. Hokkaido
51. Tokyo

HISTORY & GEOGRAPHY 408

ALTERNATE LIFEPAC TEST

NAME _____

DATE _____

SCORE _____

Put a *C* if the item best describes or is from Cuba, an *I* if it best describes Iceland, and a *J* if it is Japan (2 points each answer).

1. _____ part of Europe

2. _____ part of Asia

3. _____ part of North America

4. _____ first woman president

5. _____ Althing

6. _____ Honshu

7. _____ Bullet train

8. _____ near the Arctic Circle

9. _____ culture came from China

10. _____ sugar is the most important export

11. _____ sheep are the most important farm animal

12. _____ Mount Fuji

13. _____ Isle of Youth

14. _____ communist

15. _____ Vikings

16. _____ ruled by Spain

17. _____ ruled by Denmark

18. _____ fertile soil and many mineral resources

19. _____ the people love natural beauty and order in their crowded land

20. _____ Surtsey

21. _____ near the Caribbean Sea

22. _____ near the Sea of Okhotsk

23. _____ near the Yucatán Passage

24. _____ has huge supply of geothermal and hydroelectric power

25. _____ Shinto and Buddhism are important religions.

Write *true* or *false* on the blank (1 point each answer).

26. _____ Islands can be created by volcanoes.

27. _____ Cuba sells high quality goods all over the world.

28. _____ Most of Cuba is covered with mountains.

29. _____ The interior of Iceland is very crowded with people.

30. _____ Barrier islands are created by coral reefs.

31. _____ The Westman Islands are part of the West Indies.

32. _____ Communist countries are usually poor.

33. _____ A samurai was a Japanese soldier under the feudal government.

34. _____ There are no glaciers on Iceland.

35. _____ A saga is a book about the Revolution in Cuba.

36. _____ Cuban people cannot freely worship God.

37. _____ Great Britain is an important island in Asia.

38. _____ Cuba was discovered by the Vikings.

39. _____ Japanese teach their children to be independent and different from everyone else.

Choose the correct word from the list to complete each sentence (3 points each answer).

Havana   Denmark   Madagascar
Greenland   Meiji   Fidel Castro
Reykhavík   Tokyo   Antilles
Nippon   Hokkaido   Florida

40. _____ is the capital of Cuba.

41. _____ is the name of a Japanese emperor and the time in which he ruled.

42. The Straits of _____ are just north of Cuba.

43. _____ is the capital of Iceland.

44. _____ is the world's largest island.

45. The _____ Strait is between Iceland and Greenland.

46. _____ is a large island on the east coast of Africa.

47. _____ was the dictator of Cuba.

48. _____ means "source of the sun."

49. Cuba is a part of the _____ Islands.

50. _____ is one of the four main Japanese islands.

51. _____ is the capital of Japan.

HISTORY & GEOGRAPHY 409

Unit 9: North America

TEACHER NOTES

MATERIALS NEEDED FOR LIFEPAC	
Required	Suggested
• dictionary • encyclopedia • atlas, maps, globe • crayons, colored pencils or markers (the reference materials can be either in book or online formats)	• available materials about your state; Note: Free or inexpensive materials may be obtained through state offices. Check the yellow pages or online for addresses of Chambers of Commerce, Department of Tourism, or the State Department. • wall-size maps (political, relief) of the United States

ADDITIONAL LEARNING ACTIVITIES

Section 1: Geography of North America

1. Make a relief map of the United States showing the natural regions. Paint each region a different color and write up a map key to explain the coloring.

2. Draw a precipitation map of the United States, color, and make a map key.

Section 2: Northern Countries

1. If there is a historical museum in your town, a field trip should be planned.

2. Discuss the differences in the founding of each of the countries of North America.

3. Have a history day when each student dresses up in the style of a particular historical person or event such as an Indian, colonial woman, cowboy, soldier, or even a flapper (1920s woman). Student should have a short oral report prepared to explain the historical setting of his costume or a play could be written about an interesting historical event and given on this day.

4. Discuss the different foods from countries in North America. Have students bring a favorite food from one of the countries.

Section 3: Southern Countries

1. Discuss the similarities and differences between Mexico and Central America.

2. Have the students create a diary of an imaginary cruise to each of the countries in the West Indies. Information should include sights, activities and key aspects of each country.

Administer the LIFEPAC Test.

> The test is to be administered in one session. Give no help except with directions.
> Evaluate the tests and review areas where the students have done poorly.
> Review the pages and activities that stress the concepts tested.
> If necessary, administer the Alternate LIFEPAC Test.

INDEPENDENT STUDY ACTIVITY: YOUR STATE

This purpose for this project is to learn where the people in your state came from and why they came. You will also study about the Native Americans, the Indians, of your area. Place all of your work in a folder.

For some of the activities you can use the LIFEPAC. For others you will use an encyclopedia, an atlas, online resources, or other materials.

Follow all directions carefully.

The people. The land now occupied by the United States was once occupied by Native Americans whose way of life was much different than ours. For these activities you will need to find information about the Indians who live or lived in your state.

Activity 1: In an encyclopedia or other book about your state, find the name(s) of the Indian tribes that lived in your state. Write a one- or two-page report about these Native Americans. Include something about each of these items:
(1) Shelter, (2) food, (3) ceremonies, and (4) crafts.

Activity 2: Draw a picture, make a collage, a diorama, or some other project about the Indians of your state. Show it to your class.

Activity 3: Write a paragraph about these Indians today. Include where they live and how their lives are different.

The past. Some areas of the country were settled early, others later. These areas were settled by many nationalities. These activities will give you a chance to learn about the earliest settlers in your state.

Activity 4: Copy and complete these sentences on lined paper.

1.   The first settlers to come to _____ were _____
           (your state)
     _____

2.   The Indians came here to _____ .

3.   In _____ _____ became a state.
           (year)   (your state)

4.   Before _____ was a state it was a
                           (your state)
     _____ .
       (colony, territory, commonwealth)

Activity 5: People from many lands came to the United States. Many nationalities stayed together. Find out what nationalities may have settled in your state. Write a paragraph or two about them. Include some special customs they might have.

The present. Now that transportation is fast and easy, many products are moved from one state to another. Some states are quite famous for the special things they produce. Cheese from Wisconsin, automobiles from Michigan, and oranges from California and Florida are some examples.

Activity 6: On an outline map of your state draw some of the products your state shares with the rest of the country.

Activity 7: Choose one of your state's products. Make a poster advertising it.

Activity 8: Every state has some important people in its history. Choose someone interesting from your state's history and write a report about that person.

Activity 9: Review the material in your folder. Give the folder to your teacher.

ANSWER KEYS

SECTION 1

1.1	Cordillera
1.2	Laurentian, Appalachian
1.3	Great Basin
1.4	Sierra Madre
1.5	Rocky
1.6	Canadian Shield
1.7	Superior
1.8	Any order:
	Superior, Michigan, Huron, Erie, and Ontario
1.9	Atlantic, Great
1.10	Mississippi
1.11	Coastal
1.12	Mexico
1.13	e
1.14	b
1.15	k
1.16	i
1.17	f
1.18	a
1.19	g
1.20	j
1.21	h
1.22	c
1.23	d
1.24	Pacific
1.25	Atlantic
1.26	Atlantic
1.27	Atlantic
1.28	Pacific
1.29	Pacific
1.30	Atlantic
1.31	Atlantic
1.32	false
1.33	true
1.34	false
1.35	false
1.36	false
1.37	true
1.38	true
1.39	true
1.40	b
1.41	e
1.42	f
1.43	c
1.44	d
1.45	d
1.46	a

SELF TEST 1

1.01	I
1.02	B
1.03	V
1.04	Z
1.05	H
1.06	U
1.07	C
1.08	F
1.09	S
1.010	X
1.011	A
1.012	W
1.013	D
1.014	J
1.015	Q
1.016	M
1.017	K
1.018	R
1.019	O
1.020	P
1.021	N
1.022	T
1.023	Y
1.024	E
1.025	L
1.026	G
1.027	Great Basin
1.028	Greenland
1.029	Mexico
1.030	United States
1.031	Canada
1.032	Sierra Madre
1.033	Rocky
1.034	West Indies
1.035	Laurentian
1.036	true
1.037	false
1.038	false
1.039	true

SECTION 2

2.1	c		2.52	Mason-Dixon
2.2	d		2.53	Confederate
2.3	a		2.54	West Virginia
2.4	b		2.55	Washington, District of Columbia
2.5	e		2.56	Any order: Maryland, Virginia
2.6	f		2.57	Coastal
2.7	Eric the Red		2.58	Piedmont
2.8	Hans Egede		2.59	Ozark
2.9	Thule		2.60	Ohio
2.10	ice		2.61	Mississippi
2.11	Denmark		2.62	Teacher check
2.12	Teacher check		2.63	false
2.13	James Bay		2.64	false
2.14	Great Bear Lake		2.65	false
2.15	Ontario		2.66	true
2.16	ten		2.67	true
2.17	federal		2.68	true
2.18	second		2.69	false
2.19	Any order: Alberta, Saskatchewan, Manitoba		2.70	false
2.20	Either order: Great Bear Lake, Great Slave Lake		2.71	Teacher check
			2.72	false
2.21	Arctic, Atlantic		2.73	true
2.22	Nunavut, Inuit		2.74	true
2.23	false		2.75	true
2.24	true		2.76	false
2.25	true		2.77	false
2.26	true		2.78	true
2.27	true		2.79	true
2.28	false		2.80	Teacher check
2.29	false		2.81	Rocky
2.30	false		2.82	Colorado
2.31	false		2.83	Great Basin
2.32	true		2.84	Great Salt
2.33	true		2.85	Grand
2.34	Teacher check		2.86	Teacher check
2.35	h		2.87	false
2.36	d		2.88	true
2.37	f		2.89	false
2.38	b		2.90	true
2.39	a		2.91	false
2.40	c		2.92	false
2.41	e		2.93	true
2.42	g		2.94	true
2.43	powerful		2.95	false
2.44	contiguous			
2.45	melting pot			
2.46	wider			
2.47	rocky			
2.48	Appalachian			
2.49	factories			
2.50	Long			
2.51	Teacher check			

STATES AND CAPITALS TEST KEY

1. Alaska, Juneau
2. Hawaii, Honolulu
3. Washington, Olympia
4. Oregon, Salem
5. California, Sacramento
6. Nevada, Carson City
7. Idaho, Boise
8. Montana, Helena
9. Wyoming, Cheyenne
10. Utah, Salt Lake City
11. Colorado, Denver
12. Arizona, Phoenix
13. New Mexico, Santa Fe
14. North Dakota, Bismarck
15. South Dakota, Pierre
16. Nebraska, Lincoln
17. Kansas, Topeka
18. Oklahoma, Oklahoma City
19. Texas, Austin
20. Minnesota, St. Paul
21. Iowa, Des Moines
22. Missouri, Jefferson City
23. Arkansas, Little Rock
24. Louisiana, Baton Rouge
25. Wisconsin, Madison
26. Illinois, Springfield
27. Michigan, Lansing
28. Indiana, Indianapolis
29. Kentucky, Frankfort
30. Tennessee, Nashville
31. Mississippi, Jackson
32. Alabama, Montgomery
33. Ohio, Columbus
34. New York, Albany
35. Pennsylvania, Harrisburg
36. West Virginia, Charleston
37. Virginia, Richmond
38. North Carolina, Raleigh
39. Georgia, Atlanta
40. South Carolina, Columbia
41. Florida, Tallahassee
42. Vermont, Montpelier
43. New Hampshire, Concord
44. Maine, Augusta
45. Massachusetts, Boston
46. Connecticut, Hartford
47. Rhode Island, Providence
48. New Jersey, Trenton
49. Maryland, Annapolis
50. Delaware, Dover

SELF TEST 2

2.01 G
2.02 I
2.03 A
2.04 E
2.05 D
2.06 K
2.07 L
2.08 P
2.09 M
2.010 Q
2.011 N
2.012 C
2.013 F
2.014 J
2.015 S
2.016 H
2.017 B
2.018 T
2.019 O
2.020 R
2.021 G
2.022 C
2.023 U
2.024 U
2.025 G
2.026 U
2.027 U
2.028 C
2.029 C
2.030 G
2.031 g
2.032 c
2.033 h
2.034 j
2.035 b
2.036 d
2.037 i
2.038 e
2.039 a
2.040 f

SECTION 3

3.1	Mexico City
3.2	Spanish and Indian (Native American)
3.3	Sierra Madre
3.4	the Central Plateau
3.5	Isthmus of Techantepec and the Yucatán Peninsula
3.6	silver and petroleum
3.7	Maya and Aztec
3.8	1821
3.9	the Revolution
3.10	Teacher check
3.11	Spanish and Indian
3.12	mountains
3.13	Atlantic
3.14	volcanoes
3.15	rain forests
3.16	Mayan
3.17	Spain
3.18	The U.S. helped Panama to become independent because Columbia would not accept America's offer for the land to build a canal.
3.19	crops
3.20	Bahamas and Antilles
3.21	Any order: Cuba, Puerto Rico, Hispaniola, and Jamaica
3.22	Windward and Leeward Islands
3.23	African and European
3.24	Santo Domingo
3.25	twenty-four
3.26	farming
3.27	false
3.28	true
3.29	true
3.30	true
3.31	true
3.32	false
3.33	false

SELF TEST 3

3.01	P
3.02	H
3.03	E
3.04	C
3.05	T
3.06	J
3.07	M
3.08	A
3.09	N
3.010	G
3.011	B
3.012	S
3.013	O
3.014	D
3.015	F
3.016	K
3.017	I
3.018	L
3.019	Q
3.020	R
3.021	M
3.022	C
3.023	W
3.024	C
3.025	M
3.026	W
3.027	M
3.028	C
3.029	W
3.030	W
3.031	false
3.032	false
3.033	false
3.034	true
3.035	false
3.036	true
3.037	false
3.038	true
3.039	true
3.040	false
3.041	true
3.042	true
3.043	true
3.044	false
3.045	false
3.046	false
3.047	true
3.048	true
3.049	true
3.050	false

LIFEPAC TEST

1. F
2. N
3. J
4. B
5. D
6. T
7. S
8. K
9. L
10. R
11. P
12. G
13. H
14. I
15. C
16. Q
17. E
18. O
19. A
20. M
21. h
22. j
23. a
24. g
25. i
26. b
27. c
28. e
29. f
30. d
31. true
32. true
33. true
34. true
35. true
36. true
37. false
38. false
39. true
40. false
41. true
42. false
43. false
44. false
45. true
46. false
47. true
48. false
49. true
50. true

ALTERNATE LIFEPAC TEST

1. E
2. Q
3. M
4. F
5. I
6. O
7. B
8. K
9. S
10. G
11. D
12. P
13. L
14. C
15. A
16. T
17. J
18. R
19. H
20. N
21. Canada
22. Quebec
23. Alaska
24. Denmark
25. Mexico
26. Hispaniola
27. West Indies
28. Mississippi
29. St. Lawrence
30. Baffin
31. g
32. b
33. c
34. a
35. h
36. i
37. d
38. e
39. f
40. j

HISTORY & GEOGRAPHY 409

ALTERNATE LIFEPAC TEST

NAME _____

DATE _____

SCORE _____

80

100

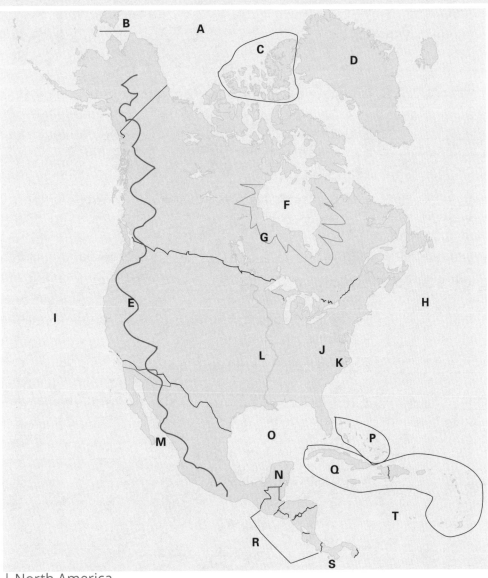

| North America

Put the best letter from the map of North America in the blank for each feature (3 points each answer).

1. _____ Cordillera
2. _____ Antilles
3. _____ Gulf of California
4. _____ Hudson Bay
5. _____ Pacific Ocean
6. _____ Gulf of Mexico
7. _____ Bering Strait
8. _____ Coastal Plains
9. _____ Isthmus of Panama
10. _____ Canadian Shield

11. _____ Greenland
12. _____ Bahamas
13. _____ Central Lowlands
14. _____ Queen Elizabeth Islands
15. _____ Arctic Ocean
16. _____ Caribbean Sea
17. _____ Appalachians
18. _____ Central America
19. _____ Atlantic Ocean
20. _____ Yucatán Peninsula

Choose the correct word to complete each sentence (2 points each answer).

Alaska   Mississippi   St. Lawrence
Canada   Mexico   West Indies
Quebec   Hispaniola   Baffin
Denmark

21. _____ is a country that is a member of the British Commonwealth.

22. _____ is a province of Canada.

23. The Aleutian islands reach from _____ toward Asia.

24. Greenland is a part of the country of _____ .

25. The Aztec civilization was in _____ .

26. _____ is an island in the West Indies.

27. _____ were the first part of North America discovered by Columbus.

28. The basin of the _____ River covers most of the center of the contiguous United States.

29. Cities on the Great Lakes are ocean ports because of the _____ Seaway.

30. _____ Island is the largest island in Canada.

Choose the best match for the following (2 points each answer).

31. _____ Greenland

32. _____ West Indies

33. _____ Canada

34. _____ United States

35. _____ Central America

36. _____ Mexico

37. _____ Canada and the U.S.

38. _____ Asia

39. _____ Superior

40. _____ Michigan

a. most powerful nation on earth

b. people are a mix of African and European ancestry

c. has both a French and British culture

d. the Great Plains are there

e. where the first North American settlers came from

f. largest fresh water lake in the world

g. people are a mix of Inuit and Viking

h. El Salvador, Nicaragua, Costa Rica

i. country is a central plateau surrounded by mountains and narrow coastal plains

j. only Great Lake completely in the U.S.

HISTORY & GEOGRAPHY 410

Unit 10: Our World in Review

TEACHER NOTES

MATERIALS NEEDED FOR LIFEPAC	
Required	Suggested
• dictionary • encyclopedia • atlas, maps, globe • crayons, colored pencils or markers (the reference materials can be either in book or online formats)	None

ADDITIONAL LEARNING ACTIVITIES

Section 1: Europe and the Explorers

1. Visit the Salvation Army in your city.

2. Review accomplishments of each explorer and Christian leader in this LIFEPAC. Write one question and answer about each one. Ask questions to a partner.

Section 2: Asia and Africa

1. Keep a bulletin board of news items about these countries.

2. Write a question and answer about each country. Ask the questions to the class for review.

Section 3: Southern Continents

1. Review on a large map the places to be reviewed in this section.

2. Same as for Section 2.

Section 4: North America, North Pole

1. Review Antarctica and the North Pole. Use maps.

2. Make a bulletin board titled, "Exploration." Use magazine pictures and newspaper items about arctic exploration.

3. Draw a picture of the team discovering the South Pole.

Administer the LIFEPAC Test.

> The test is to be administered in one session. Give no help except with directions.
> Evaluate the tests and review areas where the students have done poorly.
> Review the pages and activities that stress the concepts tested.
> If necessary, administer the Alternate LIFEPAC Test.

ANSWER KEYS

SECTION 1

1.1 - 1.9

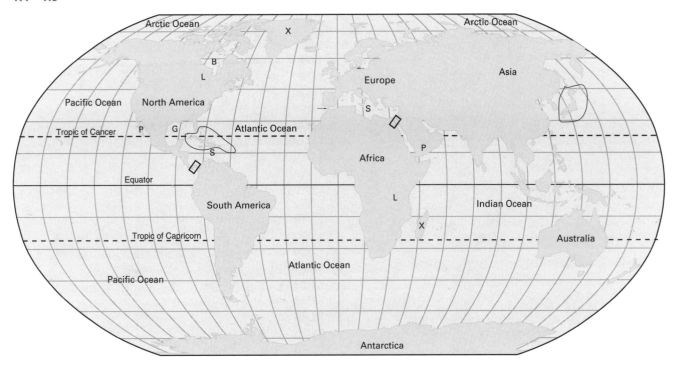

1.10	d		**1.33**	i
1.11	e		**1.34**	Mediterranean
1.12	c		**1.35**	Ural
1.13	b		**1.36**	Mediterranean; Atlantic
1.14	f		**1.37**	Teacher check
1.15	a		**1.38**	Either order: Alps, Jura
1.16	h		**1.39**	Either order: Constance, Geneva
1.17	g		**1.40**	neutral
1.18	spices		**1.41**	Ukraine; Switzerland
1.19	Spain		**1.42**	Any three:
1.20	through an air hose above the water			watches, cheese, chocolate, banking, mountains
1.21	Soviet Union		**1.43**	Breadbasket; The Steppes
1.22	Apollo		**1.44**	Cossacks
1.23	They could be reused and land like an airplane.		**1.45**	USSR; communist
			1.46	Eastern Orthodox
1.24	c		**1.47**	L
1.25	h		**1.48**	L
1.26	f		**1.49**	I
1.27	a		**1.50**	L
1.28	b		**1.51**	I
1.29	j		**1.52**	I
1.30	d		**1.53**	I
1.31	g		**1.54**	L
1.32	e			

1.55	I
1.56	L
1.57	L
1.58	I
1.59	I
1.60	I
1.61	L
1.62	I
1.63	I

SELF TEST 1

1.01	archipelago
1.02	globe
1.03	peasant
1.04	plateau
1.05	isthmus
1.06	neutral
1.07	fertile
1.08	landlocked
1.09	communism
1.010	strait
1.011	S
1.012	U
1.013	L
1.014	L
1.015	S
1.016	I
1.017	U
1.018	U
1.019	S
1.020	I
1.021	j
1.022	g
1.023	a
1.024	c
1.025	e
1.026	d
1.027	b
1.028	f
1.029	h
1.030	i
1.031	true
1.032	false
1.033	false
1.034	false
1.035	true

SECTION 2

2.1	Teacher check		**2.32**	N
2.2	Any order: Mongolia, China		**2.33**	N
2.3	Saudi Arabia		**2.34**	Tropic of Cancer
2.4	Teacher check		**2.35**	Tropic of Capricorn
2.5	Any order: Kathmandu, Tokyo		**2.36**	equator
2.6	H		**2.37**	Teacher check
2.7	I		**2.38**	Teacher check
2.8	I		**2.39**	Any order: Kinshasa, Nairobi
2.9	H		**2.40**	Africa
2.10	H		**2.41**	Suez
2.11	I		**2.42**	Nile
2.12	I		**2.43**	Victoria
2.13	H		**2.44**	Sahara
2.14	H		**2.45**	Sahel
2.15	I		**2.46**	Muslim
2.16	I		**2.47**	gold and salt
2.17	Rub´ al-Khali		**2.48**	Timbuktu
2.18	oil		**2.49**	Botswana
2.19	Muslim		**2.50**	Kalahari
2.20	camels		**2.51**	pans
2.21	Mongolia, Himalaya		**2.52**	hunter/gatherers
2.22	steppes		**2.53**	B
2.23	ger or yurt		**2.54**	C
2.24	N		**2.55**	C
2.25	J		**2.56**	C
2.26	J		**2.57**	K
2.27	J		**2.58**	B
2.28	N		**2.59**	K
2.29	N		**2.60**	C
2.30	J		**2.61**	K
2.31	J		**2.62**	C
			2.63	C
			2.64	K
			2.65	K
			2.66	K
			2.67	K

SELF TEST 2

2.01	j
2.02	i
2.03	c
2.04	h
2.05	g
2.06	b
2.07	d
2.08	e
2.09	f
2.010	a
2.011	H
2.012	J
2.013	C
2.014	K
2.015	I
2.016	K
2.017	N
2.018	I
2.019	J
2.020	N
2.021	Asia
2.022	Europe
2.023	Africa
2.024	Europe
2.025	Asia
2.026	Asia
2.027	Asia
2.028	Europe
2.029	Africa
2.030	Europe
2.031	Apollo
2.032	Iceland
2.033	London
2.034	Switzerland
2.035	*Sputnik*
2.036	Kalahari
2.037	Ukraine
2.038	Suez
2.039	Ural
2.040	Columbus

SECTION 3

3.1	Any order: Great Sandy, Gibson, Great Victoria
3.2	Tropic of Capricorn
3.3	Tasmania
3.4	Teacher check: Queen Victoria of Britain paragraph should include something about her and the British Empire
3.5	Down Under
3.6	Island
3.7	James Cook
3.8	winter
3.9	Aborigines
3.10	*Playa*
3.11	penal
3.12	Port Jackson
3.13	Either order: Sydney Harbour Bridge, Opera House
3.14	Sydneysiders
3.15	Teacher check
3.16	Any two: Brazil, Ecuador, Columbia
3.17	Any two: Chile, Paraguay, Brazil, Argentina
3.18	Teacher check
3.19	south
3.20	Suriname
3.21	Isthmus of Panama
3.22	The cold water on the coast that comes from Antarctica.
3.23	The people use plastic sheets to catch fog. It forms drops of water that fall into pans underneath.
3.24	The ships can come up the Amazon River to Iquinto.
3.25	terraces, roads, cities, and palaces
3.26	knotted ropes used to keep records
3.27	They wanted the Inca's gold and silver.
3.28	He kidnapped the Inca, forced him to pay a huge amount to be released, and then killed him.
3.29	Either order: Spanish, Indian
3.30	second, water
3.31	rubber
3.32	slash, burn
3.33	Pampas
3.34	Tierra del Fuego
3.35	Patagonia
3.36	European
3.37	gaucho
3.38	The soil is not fertile. It only grows crops for a few years and then it is left empty.

3.39	It sold wheat and beef to Europe.
3.40	The military taking over the government and debt
3.41	Teacher check
3.42	north (<u>everything</u> is always north of the South Pole)
3.43	ice shelves
3.44	b
3.45	d
3.46	a
3.47	c
3.48	true
3.49	false
3.50	false
3.51	false
3.52	true
3.53	false
3.54	true

SELF TEST 3

3.01	S
3.02	Ant
3.03	B
3.04	P
3.05	P
3.06	Arg
3.07	B
3.08	Arg
3.09	Arg
3.010	S
3.011	Ant
3.012	S
3.013	S
3.014	B
3.015	Ant
3.016	Europe
3.017	Asia
3.018	Europe
3.019	Africa
3.020	South America
3.021	Europe
3.022	Africa
3.023	Asia
3.024	Africa
3.025	Asia
3.026	true
3.027	true
3.028	true
3.029	false
3.030	true
3.031	false
3.032	true
3.033	true
3.034	false
3.035	false
3.036	false
3.037	true
3.038	true
3.039	true
3.040	true
3.041	true
3.042	false
3.043	true
3.044	false
3.045	false

SECTION 4

4.1	Teacher check
4.2	Teacher check
4.3	Teacher check
4.4	Atlantic
4.5	Teacher check
4.6	third
4.7	Canadian Shield
4.8	Europeans
4.9	Bering Strait
4.10	Greenland
4.11	Greenland
4.12	an ice cap
4.13	Viking
4.14	second
4.15	British
4.16	fur
4.17	never did
4.18	south
4.19	b
4.20	c
4.21	g
4.22	f
4.23	a
4.24	e
4.25	d
4.26	h
4.27	false
4.28	false
4.29	true
4.30	false
4.31	false
4.32	true
4.33	Any order: Belize, El Salvador, Guatemala, Honduras, Nicaragua, Costa Rica, Panama
4.34	Either order: Bahamas, Antilles
4.35	mix of European and African called Creole
4.36	Any order: Jamaica, Puerto Rico, Cuba, Hispaniola
4.37	twenty-four
4.38	Any order: sugar, tobacco
4.39	Spanish-American War
4.40	communist; Fidel Castro
4.41	Havana
4.42	They can go to jail.
4.43	North
4.44	Arctic; North America
4.45	tundra
4.46	Lapps

4.47	Any order: North America, Asia
4.48	Northwest, Roald Amundsen
4.49	Robert Peary
4.50	Richard Byrd; *Nautilus*

CROSSWORD REVIEW

Across:	Down:
2. Kinshasa	1. Nairobi
4. Kiev	2. Kathmandu
5. Brasilia	3. Nuuk
8. Buenos Aires	6. Washington
10. Havana	7. Reykjavik
13. Victoria	9. Ottawa
15. Mexico City	11. Lima
16. London	12. Bern
	14. Tokyo

SELF TEST 4

4.01	Cuba		**4.021**	j
4.02	M		**4.022**	b
4.03	CA		**4.023**	d
4.04	CA		**4.024**	h
4.05	G		**4.025**	e
4.06	WI		**4.026**	a
4.07	M		**4.027**	i
4.08	Can		**4.028**	f
4.09	US		**4.029**	London
4.010	US		**4.030**	Ukraine
4.011	Can		**4.031**	Japan
4.012	G		**4.032**	Nepal
4.013	CA		**4.033**	Sydney
4.014	Cuba		**4.034**	Kenya
4.015	Cuba		**4.035**	Hong Kong
4.016	Any order: Europe, Asia, North America		**4.036**	Istanbul
4.017	Hudson Bay		**4.037**	Peru
4.018	Northwest Passage		**4.038**	Iceland
4.019	c			
4.020	g			

LIFEPAC TEST

1. Canada
2. Peru
3. Brazil
4. Japan
5. London
6. Switzerland
7. Greenland
8. Argentina
9. Cuba
10. Central America
11. Istanbul
12. Iceland
13. Kenya
14. Mexico
15. Sydney
16. West Indies
17. Congo
18. Hong Kong
19. Ukraine
20. Nepal
21. South America
22. North America
23. Asia
24. Australia
25. Antarctica
26. Europe
27. Africa
28. false
29. false
30. false
31. true
32. false
33. true

ALTERNATE LIFEPAC TEST

1. Nepal
2. Ukraine
3. Hong Kong
4. Central America
5. Istanbul
6. Congo
7. West Indies
8. Iceland
9. Sydney
10. Kenya
11. Mexico
12. Canada
13. Cuba
14. Argentina
15. Peru
16. Greenland
17. Japan
18. London
19. Switzerland
20. Brazil
21. e
22. c
23. b
24. h
25. j
26. i
27. d
28. g
29. a
30. f

HISTORY & GEOGRAPHY 410

ALTERNATE LIFEPAC TEST

NAME _____

DATE _____

SCORE _____

80
100

Using the clues, choose the correct place from the list (4 points each answer).

London	Iceland	Ukraine	Switzerland
Istanbul	Nepal	Kenya	Hong Kong
Congo	Japan	Peru	Argentina
Brazil	Sydney	Mexico	Greenland
Canada	West Indies	Cuba	Central America

1. _____ Himalaya Mountains; one of the poorest countries on earth; Asia; main religion—Hindu

2. _____ Europe; grassland country; steppes; capital—Kiev; was part of the Union of Soviet Socialist Republics

3. _____ Asian seaport; includes Victoria, Kowloon, and the New Territories; many people are hard-working Chinese refugees

4. _____ North America; Isthmus of Panama; Maya Indians; Belize was a British colony, the rest were Spanish

5. _____ European and Asian seaport; Constantinople; capital of the Ottoman Empire; people are Turkish Muslims

6. _____ Africa; colony of Belgium; rain forest; capital—Kinshasa; dictator Joseph Mobutu stole until country was very poor

7. _____ North America; two archipelagoes—Bahamas and Antilles; culture a mix of different European and African nations

8. _____ Europe; island nation; *Althing*—world's oldest parliament; export mainly fish and wool; speak an old Norse language

9. _____ Australian seaport; landing place for the First Fleet; penal colony; Port Jackson; nation part of British Commonwealth

10. _____ Africa; grassland country—savanna; famous for safaris; Swahili culture/language came from city-states on coast

11. _____ North American country; Spanish colony; leader in silver and oil production; heartland—Central Plateau; dry land

12. _____ largest North American country; French and British heritage; federation of 10 provinces and 2 territories; capital—Ottawa

13. _____ North American island country; communist; Fidel Castro, dictator; exports sugar and tobacco; capital—Havana

14. _____ South America; grassland country—Pampas; Tierra del Fuego; capital—Buenos Aires; Patagonia; exports beef and wheat

15. _____ South America; Andes Mountains; Inca Empire; source of the Amazon River; capital—Lima

16. _____ North America; part of Denmark; island; covered by an ice cap; mainly north of the Arctic Circle; people Inuit/Viking

17. _____ Asian archipelago nation; *shogun* ruled for the emperor for many years; capital—Tokyo; people love nature and beauty

18. _____ European seaport; Great Britain's capital; the City was the old part built by the Romans; Thames River

19. _____ Europe; Alps and Jura Mountains; Lakes Geneva and Constance; cantons fought for independence; today, is neutral

20. _____ South America; Amazon rain forest; colony of Portugal; rubber was an important product; forest being destroyed

Match these items (2 points each answer).

21. _____ desert in North Africa, largest on earth

22. _____ desert in Asia, Mongolia

23. _____ Island Continent, center is mostly desert

24. _____ desert in South America, Chile

25. _____ most southern continent; an icy desert

26. _____ America's first stage in space program

27. _____ the tropic line north of the equator

28. _____ the tropic line south of the equator

29. _____ desert, has the Great Basin, Death Valley, Mohave Desert

30. _____ Arctic people of America and Asia

a. American Southwest

b. Australia

c. Gobi

d. Cancer

e. Sahara

f. Inuit (Eskimo)

g. Capricorn

h. Atacama

i. Mercury

j. Antarctica